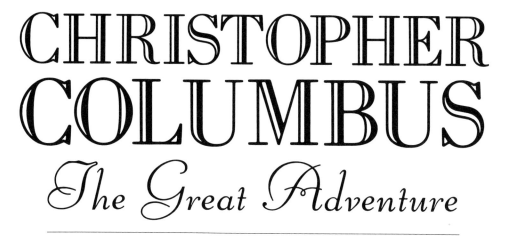

# CHRISTOPHER COLUMBUS
## *The Great Adventure*

### AND HOW WE KNOW ABOUT IT

## DELNO C. WEST & JEAN M. WEST

ILLUSTRATED WITH
PRINTS, MAPS, AND PHOTOGRAPHS

ATHENEUM · 1991 · NEW YORK

MAXWELL MACMILLAN CANADA

TORONTO

MAXWELL MACMILLAN INTERNATIONAL

NEW YORK  OXFORD  SINGAPORE  SYDNEY

Illustration credits

Genoa State Archives 5; National Maritime Museum, London 16; National Gallery of Art 25; Bodleian Library, Oxford 32; Princeton University Library 37, 38; Mariner's Museum 42, 48; Toledo Museum of Art 91

Chapter opening illustrations:

xii  An engraving of Columbus from a sixteenth-century book by Capriolo

20  *Christopher Columbus,* painted by Sebastiano de Piombo in the sixteenth century. Courtesy of The Metropolitan Museum of Art, Gift of J. Pierpont Morgan, 1900.

48  *Columbus Leaving Palos,* by Joaquin Sorolla y Bastida. Courtesy of the Mariner's Museum, Newport News, Virginia

92  A portrait of Columbus painted in the sixteenth century, artist unknown. Courtesy Museo Civico, Como.

Atheneum
Macmillan Publishing Company
866 Third Avenue
New York, NY 10022

Maxwell Macmillan Canada, Inc.
1200 Elington Avenue East
Suite 200
Don Mills, Ontario M3C 3N1

Macmillan Publishing Company is part of the Maxwell Communication Group of Companies.

First edition

Printed in the United States of America

10  9  8  7  6  5  4  3  2  1

Design by Trish Parcell

The text of this book is set in 12/16 Loren.

Library of Congress Cataloging-in-Publication Data

West, Delno C., 1936–
    Christopher Columbus: the great adventure and how we know about it / by Delno C. West and Jean M. West.—1st ed.
      p.   cm.
    Summary: Describes the early life and studies of Christopher Columbus, his search for support of a voyage across the Atlantic, and his experiences in the New World.
    ISBN 0-689-31433-7
    1. Columbus, Christopher—Juvenile literature.  2. Explorers—American—Biography—Junvenile literature.  3. Explorers—Spain—Biography—Juvenile literature.
    4. America—Discovery and exploration—Spanish—Juvenile literature.
    [1. Columbus, Christopher.  2. Explorers.  3. America—Discovery and exploration—Spanish.]
    I. West, Jean M.  II. Title.
E111.W47   1991
970.01'5'092—dc20
[B]
[92]
                  90–936
                  CIP

*This book is dedicated to our grandchildren*
*Crystal Christine Corbally*
*and*
*Phillip John Corbally III*

# Contents

# CHAPTER ONE

# The Dream Begins

The calm of the morning was broken by the sound of thunder to the
north and east. But it was not thunder; it was cannon fire! An enemy
fleet was coming fast toward the merchant convoy. Christopher Columbus, a twenty-five-year-old common deckhand, probably heard
the sounds just as he finished his morning meal. Earlier, the cabin
boy had sung the morning ceremony for the sailors:

> *Blessed by the light of day*
> *and the Holy Cross we say;*
> *and the Lord of Veritie*
> *and the Holy Trinity. . . .*

After the boy finished the song, the crew had assembled on deck to
recite the Paternoster and Ave Maria. They concluded with the sailor's
prayer:

> *God give us good days, good voyage, good*
> *passage to the ship, sir captain and master*
> *and good company, so let there be a good voyage;*
> *many good days may God grant your graces,*
> *gentlemen of the afterguard and gentlemen forward.*

After the brief service, the crew ate their breakfast of salted fish and bread.

It was the year 1476, and Christopher was at last sailing on the great Ocean Sea, as the Atlantic Ocean was called in the fifteenth century. The coast of Europe lay to the distant east, and to the west the Ocean Sea stretched beyond the horizon. Although he was only a deckhand on this trip Christopher dreamed that someday he would be the captain of his own ship. His training as a sailor was advancing, and with this trip he would gain experience sailing on the open Ocean Sea.

Christopher Columbus was sailing with a small merchant fleet that had left the port of Noli, Italy, on May 31, 1476. They were carrying goods to trade in Lisbon, Portugal; London, England; and Flanders in Belguim. Columbus had signed on with the crew of the *Bechalla*, a heavy old cargo ship.

Christopher had been eager to go with the fleet because it would take him out beyond the Mediterranean Sea and into the Ocean Sea to the west. The trip might be dangerous because Europe was at war. Christopher's city of Genoa, Italy, was not involved, but any merchant fleet could be attacked. Furthermore, any trip into the Ocean Sea held the prospect of danger.

Now the worst fears of the crew were realized. The merchant fleet was being attacked by French warships. The ships advanced and retreated all day, firing on one another and maneuvering to come near enough to grapple.

Once two ships were within a few feet of each other, the sailors could throw the huge iron grappling hooks across the water to the enemy ship and pull the vessels together. Once the ships were tied together, the crews of each ship would board the other. There would be a fight on the decks with swords, muskets, clubs, and also with bare hands.

The *Bechalla* finally was able to grapple with one of the French warships in the late afternoon. Sailors from both ships flooded onto the decks to fight. Bullets whistled through the air. Swords flashed in the bright sunlight. Christopher joined in the fighting. Fires were started on both ships. Many of his companions fell over the rails into the sea. In a struggle with one of the French sailors, Christopher may have taken a cut on his thigh from an enemy's sword.

Before long, the fires were raging out of control, and sailors from both ships stopped fighting and tried to put out the blazes before both ships sank. It was a hopeless effort. Finally, the crews from both ships abandoned their vessels and jumped into the ocean. Many of the men drowned.

Christopher was able to grab a heavy oar floating by, and he held on. He was a good swimmer, and his muscles were in top shape. Years later, he told his son Ferdinand that with God's help he made it to shore because God had a great destiny for him.

The six-mile swim to shore took several hours. He finally was able to crawl up onto the beach of the southern coast of Portugal. The people who lived nearby helped him over the sand. They gave him food and drink, wrapped him in warm blankets, and led him to a place where he could sleep after the long ordeal.

Christopher Columbus was born around 1451 near the city of Genoa, Italy. He was the oldest of five children, four boys and one girl. He and two of his brothers, Giovanni and Bartholomew, had a little boat that they sailed in the Bay of Genoa. Bianchinetta, his sister, and Giacomo, his baby brother, were too young to go along. The three brothers would sail out to the small islands in the bay and camp out overnight. They would fish and swim. They liked to race the other boats back to the docks.

His father, Domenico, was a weaver and cloth merchant. His mother, Susanna, worked in the store with his father. Everyone in his family helped in the shop. Christopher's job was to card the wool by running a rough comb through the raw wool in order to get out the impurities. Neither Bianchinetta nor Giacomo worked, for they were still too little.

Genoa is an ancient city on the western coast of Italy. In Christopher's day, it was an exciting port, with sailors from all over the Mediterranean Sea crowding the streets. There were Moors from North Africa, Arabs from the east, Spaniards and Portuguese from the west,

# How Do We Know about Columbus's Early Life?

Historians work with many kinds of documents that have survived from the past. Since most people could not read or write in the fifteenth century, they would go to a notary (a person who could read and write) to have important documents recorded. Notarial records, like the one above, help confirm that Christopher, the son of Domenico, was born in Genoa.

Christopher, who improved his abilities to read and write when he was about thirty years old, left us a ships' log, essays, letters, memoranda, a will, and notes in the margins of the books he read. Governments kept records of court activities, the king's decisions, and other matters. Columbus's friends and acquaintances wrote about him both during his lifetime and after he died.

One of his sons, Ferdinand, wrote a biography of his father. He based it on his father's papers and on remembrances of long conversations with him. An acquaintance, the Bishop Bartolomé de las Casas, also included a lengthy biography of Columbus in his *History of the Indies.* Las Casas used Columbus's ships' logs, letters, and notes to write this part of his history. So there are many written sources that tell about the famous mariner.

We do not know very much about his life before the first voyage of discovery of the New World, however. Columbus did not consider the events of his early years important enough to record. Occasionally, he mentions something that happened, such as his voyage to Iceland or seeing the bodies washed up at Galway, as these events were important to his ideas for discovery. Mostly, he recorded only those things that helped to prove his beliefs or that had a direct bearing upon his "Enterprise of the Indies," as he called his great adventure.

Documents, often, do not survive the ravages of time. War, fire, earthquake, some other disaster, or uncaring people will destroy them. For exam-

and even blacks from lower Africa. Christopher and his friends sometimes would sit below the window of the wine seller's shop and listen to the tales of the sea told by the sailors drinking inside.

Christopher and his friends all worked in their fathers' shops. They ple, we know very little about the nine years Columbus spent at Lisbon. This is in part because Columbus himself did not leave us much information about these years. Other documents, such as government and notarial records, were destroyed by the great earthquake at Lisbon in 1755. Some of these records may have contained information about Christopher, perhaps recording his negotiations with the king.

Historians also depend on archaeological findings to explain events. Ships wrecked during the fifteenth and sixteenth centuries can be recovered by underwater archaeologists. These give us information about the technology available to Columbus. Clothing, weapons, utensils, armor, furniture, and other artifacts that survived from those times give the historian some idea of what daily life was like. The words to the song and prayer aboard ship at the beginning of this chapter are those recorded by Eugenio de Salazar, a traveler aboard a ship to the New World in the sixteenth century.

*This document, dated 4 February 1477, is from the city of Genoa, Italy. It appoints Domenico Columbus as "keeper of Olivella Tower" in that city. Such documents verify that Columbus lived in Genoa as a youth. (Genoa State Archives)*

went to a small school in an alley set up by the weavers' guild. School was only for a few hours a day because the boys were needed to work most of the time. At school, the boys learned to do some arithmetic and to read and to write a little in Latin, at least enough to carry on business and to understand the services in church. Girls never went to school.

In the late afternoons, when the work in the shops was finished, sometimes Christopher and the other boys joined together to play. In a favorite game of the times, one boy ran with a melon through the streets while the other boys tried to catch him and take the melon away. Most of the time, though, he and his brothers preferred to take a little boat out into the bay.

Domenico was more than just a weaver. He was also a cloth merchant who had to travel from Genoa to buy wool to turn into cloth. At one time, he also owned a wine shop. He was a businessman in a day when merchants were becoming prominent members of society. Christopher, in a sense, followed his father's path as a merchant, but he would be more interested in importing goods by ship than in manufacturing cloth. Where and when he came to love the sea, we do not know. But when he became an adult, he became a merchant seaman commanding his own ship.

It was probably from his father that he learned to carry on business, and it was probably his father who introduced him to the trade of a merchant seaman. When Christopher was fourteen, he accompanied his father on a voyage to buy wool. They sailed along the Italian and French coasts for several days. Christopher probably watched the sailors with great interest, for it is evident that he fell in love with sailing. After this voyage, Domenico let Christopher accompany him on trading expeditions aboard ship whenever possible. It is very likely that Christopher began to learn the many tasks of a seaman on these coastal voyages.

Christopher grew into an athletic young man, tall and solidly built, as he gained valuable training sailing the coastal waters off Italy. His dream, however, as his son Ferdinand tells us, was to sail in larger ships out into the waters of the Mediterranean Sea and maybe some-day into the Ocean Sea. He dreamed of going to far-off places.

Exactly when Christopher first went to sea as an actual sailor is not really known. Two trips into the Mediterranean Sea are recorded, but historians are uncertain which was the first. Christopher's first oppor-

# Where Was Columbus Born?

Since Christopher Columbus was such an important person, many countries have tried to claim him as a native son. Writers have tried to prove that he was born in many places other than Genoa, Italy. It has been claimed that he was born in Greece, Spain, Portugal, Switzerland, and on various islands in the Mediterranean and Atlantic. Sometimes these claims arose from errors based on name similarities. At other times, misplacing his birthplace has been the result of wishful thinking and sometimes of outright fraud. One writer, for example, claimed that Colombo was the alias used by an exiled Byzantine prince on the island of Chios and that this was Christopher Columbus, who left the island and settled in Genoa.

Other writers have claimed that he was Jewish and that he and his family had converted to Christianity. These claims are based on Columbus's tendency to quote frequently from Old Testament Scriptures in the Bible. They have rationalized that Christopher's voyage across the Ocean Sea was really an attempt to find a new homeland for the Jews, who were being persecuted in Europe at this time.

All of these efforts have failed because there is too much historical evidence that he was born in Genoa, Italy, of Christian, Italian parents, as he himself stated.

tunity to cross the Mediterranean Sea probably came just after his twentieth birthday. René of Anjou commissioned Genoese ships to sail to Tunis in North Africa and fight the Barbary pirates, who were sending their fast corsairs (fighting ships) against the king's merchant ships. Christopher signed on immediately as a deckhand. The battle with the pirates never took place, but the trip got Christopher to North Africa and across the Mediterranean Sea for the first time.

The next year, he sailed on another adventure. The city of Genoa sent an expedition to relieve its colony on the Greek island of Chios in the Aegean Sea. Chios and the Genoese colony had been attacked

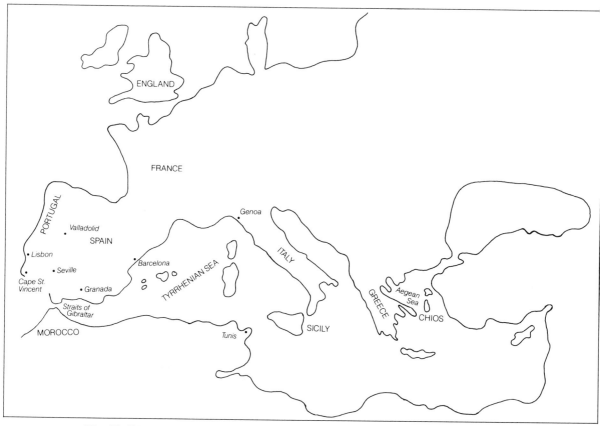

*The Mediterranean world*

by the Turks. Christopher signed on to sail with one of the richest merchant families in Genoa, the Centurione family. The Centuriones would remain his friends and supporters for the rest of his life.

It was a long voyage around the boot of Italy and across the tip of Greece through some of the most difficult currents in the Mediterranean. It was on this voyage, on this large ship, that Columbus learned to steer, to judge distances at sea, to rig the large sails, and many other skills of seamanship.

The trip to Chios was successful. But when Christopher returned to Italy, he discovered everyone was talking about a plan to send a merchant fleet to trade with the northern ports. This was his chance to sail into the great Ocean Sea to the west! Because he had been away, he was almost too late. Most of the ships already had all the sailors they needed. Friends told him that the old ship the *Bechalla* was to be manned mostly by sailors from his district in Genoa, and there were still jobs on board. He applied immediately and was hired as a deckhand.

Everything went well in the beginning. The merchant fleet had sailed westward across the Tyrrhenian Sea to the coast of Spain and followed the coastline to the Strait of Gibraltar. There they passed the Pillars of Hercules, rocky hills on either side of the Strait, and set their course to the north, again following the coast of Spain. They had expected to sight Cape St. Vincent that morning, but the attack of the French warships had spoiled that hope and stranded Christopher on the Portuguese coast.

Portugal was sometimes called the "end of the world" because it was the westernmost part of the continent of Europe. It faced the mighty Ocean Sea. Portuguese sailors were known to be the best in Europe. They sailed up and down the coast of Africa and as far north as the Arctic Ocean. Lisbon, the largest city and the main port, was the center for the adventure of ocean sailing. After his rescue, Colum-

## Why Did Columbus Go to Chios?

Chios was a Greek island in the Aegean Sea that was very important to Genoa and Genoese trade. Genoese merchants had captured the island in 1346 in order to guarantee a steady supply of mastic, which was produced on the tiny island. Mastic is a resin, a kind of sap, taken from a bush. After it was dried, the resin was placed in wooden kegs and shipped to Genoa, where it was used to make a medicine believed to relieve aches and to cleanse the blood. Since aspirin had not yet been discovered, everyone wanted this product that reduced pain. Today, mastic is used in paint, varnish, and chewing gum.

Christopher went along to gain sailing experience and probably for the adventure of helping to drive the Turks from the island. The Turks had captured the great trading port and former Byzantine capital, Constantinople (Istanbul today), in 1453, and they were rapidly capturing all the territory surrounding Greece.

bus made his way quickly to Lisbon, where many Genoese merchants and sailors lived.

For almost forty years, the Portuguese had been exploring the Ocean Sea. Prince Henry, called the Navigator, had built a research center at Cape St. Vincent to study the ocean, navigation, and to encourage exploration down the coast of Africa. The Portuguese hoped to find the end of Africa and sail around it into the Indian Ocean and on to India and Asia. Christopher found himself among people who could teach him new skills needed to sail the ocean. But, before settling down in Lisbon, he had another adventure.

Within a few months of his arrival there, as soon as his wound had healed, he signed on with a Portuguese ship to sail to Iceland. In his own words he described the trip:

*I sailed in the month of February in the year 1477 one hundred leagues beyond the isle of Tile [Iceland]. . . . To this island [Iceland], which is as large as England, come the English with their merchandise, especially those men of Bristol. And at the season when I was there, the sea was not frozen. . . .*

On the return trip, his ship docked in at Galway, in Ireland, where he witnessed a most unusual event. Into Galway harbor floated two boats with strange-looking dead people aboard. Columbus described their appearance:

*Men of Cathay [China], which is toward the Orient, have come here. We have seen many remarkable things, especially in Galway of Ireland. A man and a woman of extraordinary appearance in two boats adrift.*

Their faces, he tells us, were flat, and he believed that they had drifted across the Ocean Sea from China. They were probably Laplanders or Finns, however, who had been forced out to sea by a storm and had died. Their boats then had drifted across the North Sea, finally coming to rest near Galway. It really did not matter from where they

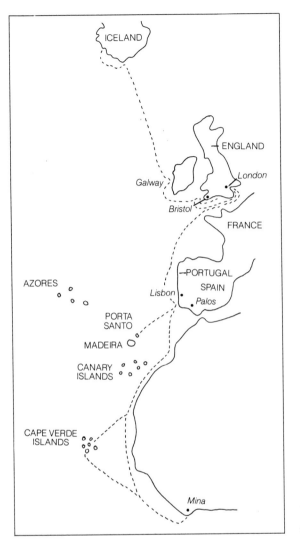

*Western Europe with Near Ocean Sea*

had come. What mattered was that Christopher believed their little boats had floated across the ocean.

Two important things occurred on this trip that were to have lasting influence upon Christopher Columbus. First, by going to Iceland, he had sailed far north into the Ocean Sea. He may even have heard Icelandic sagas, stories based on fact and myth, about the lands to the west, which had long ago been discovered by Vikings. The second influence was those two boats from "China." To Columbus, they had to have crossed the mighty Ocean Sea! Such an event meant that there had to be proper wind and ocean currents to carry vessels across the ocean. All he had to do was find those currents.

He observed the winds and sea currents on his trip to Iceland, and later, when he was returning from his first voyage to the New World, he traveled far to the north because he knew that northern winds and currents would take him east.

Back in Lisbon, Christopher settled down. His brother Bartholomew had come to the city and set up a mapmaking shop. Christopher joined him as a partner. Together they learned to draw charts and maps, which they sold to sailors. More importantly, they improved their Latin, and they learned to read and write in Spanish.

At that time, all the important books were written in Latin, and Spanish was the language spoken by most merchants and seamen. Christopher loved to read and was a natural student. He began to study the Holy Bible and the writings of great geographers, mathematicians, and astronomers.

He also watched the shipbuilders as they built the new oceangoing vessels called caravels. He learned about the best sail riggings for ocean sailing, and he studied navigation. He found that he had a natural talent for navigation.

The details of Christopher Columbus's nearly nine years in Lisbon will never be known. The records have long ago been destroyed, and he gives us very little information in his own writings. We do know that he worked with his brother, and we know that he made at least one more trip out into the Ocean Sea.

In the summer of 1478, barely a year after his return from Iceland, Christopher was employed by Paolo di Negro to sail a trading ship to the Madeira Islands to purchase sugar and take it to Genoa. This may have been his first job as a ship's captain. Paolo di Negro knew of Columbus because he was a friend and agent for the Centurione family back in Genoa who had hired Columbus as a deckhand to go to Chios earlier. The trip to Madeira took him south and west into the Ocean Sea. After taking the sugar to Genoa, he returned to Lisbon the following year.

# What Did Columbus Look Like?

There are hundreds of paintings, engravings, woodcuts, and statues of Christopher Columbus, but they were all made after he died by people who never saw him. The picture below was done as an engraving for a book sometime after 1570. Tobias Stimmer used an older portrait painted early in the sixteenth century, which was owned by an Italian collector of portraits, named Paulus Jovius. The original painting was probably done in Rome by an artist who might have seen Columbus, although this is doubtful. He also could have talked with Columbus's son Ferdinand, who went to Rome from time to time. Even so, there is no guarantee that the picture is in any way accurate and looks like the mariner. Christopher's son Ferdinand described what his father looked like in the following words: "The Admiral was a well built man of more than medium stature, long face with cheeks somewhat high but neither fat nor thin. He had a big nose and his eyes were light in color; his complexion too was light, but tending toward red. In his youth, his hair was red. . . ." Other sources tell us that as a boy Columbus had freckles and that his hair turned white at about the age of thirty.

*Sixteenth-century woodcut by Tobias Stimmer (from P. Jovius, Elogia virorum bellica virtute illustrium, Basle, 1575). Since no actual portrait of Columbus exists, artists have pictured him in various ways. He is seen as a romantic dreamer, as a nobleman, as a mystic, and as a discouraged, aged man.*

Christopher was a very religious young man. He always attended church, visited shrines, and observed holy days. Even aboard ship he remained faithful to his beliefs and always read his prayer book, prayed, and attended religious services. One day while attending mass at the chapel of the small convent of St. James in Lisbon, he met Doña Felipa Perestrello e Moniz.

Felipa was living with the nuns in the convent, because her father had died, and her mother was unable to care for her. She was from the Madeira Islands far out in the Ocean Sea, to which Columbus had sailed for sugar, in 1478. Within a few months, she and Christopher were married, and they moved to the Madeira Islands, where her brother was now governor. About a year later, a son was born to them. They named him Diego.

Doña Felipa's father had had a great interest in the Ocean Sea. He had collected many notes and artifacts about its legends and mysteries. Felipa's mother gave these notes and artifacts to Christopher.

Strange items had often washed up on the beaches of Madeira and other islands. Branches from trees unknown in Europe or Africa, weeds and other plants that did not grow in Europe or Africa floated to the island shores.

At least once, Felipa's father had found a man-made artifact on the beach—a piece of wood carved in a manner he had never seen before. He knew that it had not come from Europe or Africa. Columbus's desire for the adventure of crossing the Ocean Sea was aroused after seeing his father-in-law's collection. From other people, Columbus heard tales of strange islands and land, across the sea. The evidence seemed very strong that there were lands across the great ocean. He had to go!

While in Lisbon, Christopher and his brother had studied the theories about the earth as told in the writings of the Bible and by famous ancient and medieval geographers and other scholars. In his own conclusions about the shape and size of the earth, Christopher was convinced that it could be crossed, and he calculated that he could make the voyage.

# Legends, Tales, and Mysterious Artifacts

Scholars have long suspected that Columbus, while sailing to Iceland by way of England and to the coast of Africa, may have heard stories of land beyond the Ocean Sea. Ferdinand, his son, mentions that his father had known such tales. The sailors of Bristol, England, fished off the Newfoundland Banks and told of sighting land farther to the west. In Iceland, Christopher may have heard sagas about early Viking explorations to the west such as the one about Fredis, the daughter of Eric the Red, one of the early Viking explorers and colonists on Greenland. Fredis was the first European woman on record to set foot on American shores. She led two ships to Vineland (Newfoundland) in the eleventh century in order to cut timber.

Living at Porto Santo in the Madeira Islands, Christopher noticed with interest the plants that washed up on the beaches, pieces of wood and weed that did not grow on the islands or in Europe. Such items still drift across the Atlantic Ocean today, especially after a severe storm in the Caribbean Sea. Columbus must have wondered about the origin of such strange items, and about the one man-made artifact reportedly found by his father-in-law, a carved piece of wood totally unlike anything known to Europeans. Other people living on islands in the Ocean Sea had similar tales to tell.

As Columbus continued to read the works of great geographers and scholars of the time, he learned that Europeans had long suspected that islands existed in the Ocean Sea and that strange people inhabited them. These people were called the Antipodes, and it was believed that they were deformed creatures with one eye or three legs. The ancient writers also told the tale of the mythical island of Atlantis. In Greek mythology, Atlantis was an island faraway from the known world, where life was nearly perfect and where people enjoyed a superior civilization. It was destroyed when it sank beneath the sea. In the fifteenth century, many people believed that this island civilization had existed far out in the Ocean Sea.

Columbus believed many of these legends and myths were true. He tells us: "I have searched out and studied all kinds of texts: geographies, histories, chronologies, philosophies and other subjects. . . . I have had conversations with learned men among both the laity and the clergy, Latins and Greeks, Christians and Moslems, and many others of different cultures." His son Ferdinand says of his father: "He believed this all the more [that lands existed across the Ocean Sea] because he was impressed by the many fables and stories which he heard from various persons and sailors who traded to the western islands and seas of the Azores and Madeira."

Christopher was now a ship's captain. We know that he had contracted to haul sugar from the Madeira Islands to Genoa, and he may have had other contracts to transport goods by sea. The years of sailing and learning had paid off, and he was known as one of the most honest merchant seamen and one of the best navigators in all of Europe. He had learned how to handle the new ship and the caravel, and knew what kind of supplies to take on long voyages. He had honed his skills at navigation.

Navigation is figuring out where one is in the ocean and how to get from one place to another when out of the sight of land. Today, ships have computers, electronic devices, and orbiting satellites to help them navigate, but in Christopher's time they had only a simple compass, an astrolabe, and a sextant. Although he may have had other instruments on board, Christopher probably used only the compass, which shows direction, and the astrolabe, which shows the positions

*A fifteenth-century compass and astrolabe (National Maritime Museum, London). Guidance systems were primitive in the time of Columbus. He had to rely on his compass and astrolabe to calculate his location, and on his half-hour glass for time. Columbus probably had other instruments on board, such as the quadrant and sextant, but he did not use them. These two instruments could be used effectively only on land; the rolling deck of the ship was too unstable. Today, ships are guided by computers connected to satellites, which constantly give them exact location data.*

of the stars. But with these, Columbus could sail out into the Ocean Sea, far from the sight of land, and calculate his way back.

He also had an ability to sense the currents and winds, which enabled him to find the best and fastest routes. Perhaps most important, Christopher had confidence in himself and his skills. He continued to read and study his many books about the world.

Christopher made a trip to Africa while living in Porto Santo, in the Madeira Islands. This time he sailed under the king of Portugal's flag to the Guinea coast, where the king had built a fortress at the port of São Jorge da Mina, near the equator.

Christopher was interested in the trip because he could find out for himself the answer to another mystery. Many of the books he read, and even the people with whom he talked, claimed that humans could not cross the equator because of the intense heat. Christopher soon learned that this was false, and that not only did men cross the equator, but that many people lived in those lands without harm.

While he was near the equator, Christopher made several measurements to try to estimate the distance around the entire earth. These measurements convinced him that the circumference of the globe was much smaller than it actually is. His miscalculations would be the primary reason why later scientific commissions advised against supporting his trip across the Ocean Sea.

Christopher's desire to sail the Ocean Sea became stronger the longer he lived at Porto Santo. There he could gaze for hours across the open sea to the west and wonder what was beyond. He was sure that all one had to do was sail beyond the horizon to arrive at new lands.

But what lands? All of his studies convinced him that the great continent of Asia, with its abundance of gold and spices, was but a short distance to the west. The theories he had read also speculated that there should be more islands in the Ocean Sea, and some even hinted at unknown mainlands. All one had to do, he thought, was to make the necessary arrangements, supply ships, hire crews, and one could sail to the fabled East: China, Japan, and India.

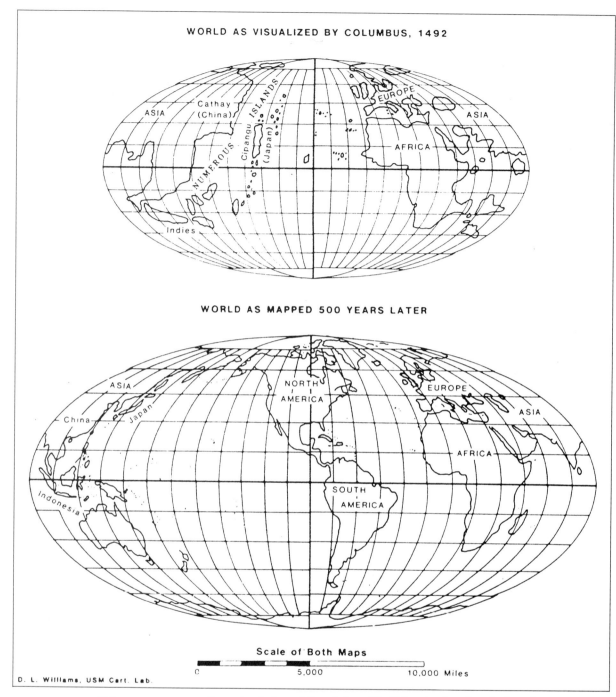

**WORLD AS VISUALIZED BY COLUMBUS, 1492**

ASIA — Cathay (China) — NUMEROUS ISLANDS — Cipangu (Japan) — Indies — EUROPE — ASIA — AFRICA

**WORLD AS MAPPED 500 YEARS LATER**

ASIA — China — Japan — NORTH AMERICA — EUROPE — ASIA — AFRICA — Indonesia — SOUTH AMERICA

**Scale of Both Maps**

0        5,000        10,000 Miles

D. L. Williams, USM Cart. Lab.

*This map compares the actual size of the globe with Columbus's miscalculated size. These two drawings demonstrate the size and configuration of the world as Columbus believed it to be and the size and configuration that we know it to be today. If the North and South American continents had not been where they are, it is doubtful that Columbus and his crew would have survived. (Map by Donald Williams.)*

## The Legend of the Unknown Pilot

Historians must judge their facts. Just because a document is old, or a legend very strong, does not mean that it is true. One of the persistent stories about Columbus, and one that even today shows up in textbooks, is the story about the "unknown pilot." The story has no basis in fact, and there is no proof that the event ever happened.

It was probably a story made up by the enemies of Columbus, who tried to discredit the importance of his discovery. By 1535, the story begins to be recorded as truth. According to this legend, the pilot of a ship going from Spain to England was blown off course by a strong storm. Fleeing before the storm, the ship sailed westward for many days until it reached new islands far across the Ocean Sea, where the natives ran about naked. The ship sailed back to Europe as soon as the weather was favorable, but all the crew died except for the ship's pilot.

The pilot, the story goes, was a friend of Christopher, so Columbus took him home to nurse him back to health. Unfortunately, the pilot died; but before he died, the pilot related his adventure to Columbus and drew him a map of these islands and showed Columbus how to reach them. This story was never mentioned by Columbus, his son, or any other record before 1535, forty-three years after Columbus sailed to the New World. Although this story has been told for centuries and is popularly believed, historians cannot find facts to show that it is really true.

On his various voyages into the Ocean Sea, he had observed the winds and currents. His instincts as a navigator told him the best route to take. He was determined to do it. The only thing stopping him was the cost of such a trip. It would be very expensive to undertake this feat, but he knew that somehow he would find the money. He would go to the king of Portugal and seek his aid.

# CHAPTER TWO

# In Search of Support

Christopher, his wife, Felipa, and their small son, Diego, returned to Portugal in the fall of 1483. Seeking support for his dream probably was not the only reason to sail to Portugal at this time. Felipa was ill, and medical facilities were many times better in Lisbon than on the remote island some eight hundred miles out in the Ocean Sea. Within the year, however, she died, leaving Columbus a widower with a small son.

Upon this return to Lisbon, Christopher found the city even more exciting than he remembered. Now young John II was the king, and everyone expected great things from the popular new leader.

Christopher wanted to see this new king and explain his plan to sail across the Ocean Sea in order to reach China. He knew that the king would be interested, for John II had frequently sent ships down the coast of Africa, trying to locate a passage to the Indian Ocean and on to Asia. Christopher believed that he had a better plan. He was sure that he could convince the king that it was shorter and cheaper to sail across the mighty Ocean Sea to reach Asia.

The young sea captain finally got his chance early in 1484. He was summoned to meet with King John II to explain his plan. He arrived at the splendid court dressed in his finest clothes. The king asked him to outline his plan and offer proof that it was possible. Christopher failed to convince the young king!

Perhaps he was too anxious. A writer of the time described the meeting as one where Christopher appeared to be too talkative, too boastful. He wrote that Christopher's ideas seemed to have little merit and that Columbus wanted too large a reward if he succeeded. Nevertheless, the king did him the courtesy of turning the idea over to a

## The Enterprise of the Indies

The "Enterprise of the Indies" was the name that Columbus gave his project to sail west in order to reach Asia. Although it looks simple to us today, in 1492 it was very complicated. Unlike today's launch of a rocket ship into outer space, where thousands of scientists have investigated every problem, where hundreds of computers assist astronauts in their travel, and where modern technology can be applied, Columbus had only himself. And there were major problems to be overcome. In the first place, the Ocean Sea was the "Sea of Darkness," untraveled and uncharted. Many superstitions existed about what was out in that ocean—sea monsters, unknown currents, strange peoples, boiling water. It was believed that perhaps one could sail into it but could not get back; the winds and currents seemed to go only one way. It was also believed by some that, if one sailed too far south, one might be roasted by the tropical sun.

Another problem was distance. Most scientists of the times calculated that it was about 11,000 miles from Portugal to Japan. Mathematical estimates about the size of the globe confirmed this figure. Columbus, using a different method of calculating the size of the earth, said it was only about 2,500 miles. Columbus was wrong, just as the scientists of the day said he was. As we now know, the huge land mass of the Western Hemisphere alone is about 3,000 miles across the ocean from Europe. Columbus may have suspected that a large land mass was out in the Ocean Sea between Europe and Asia. Many myths and legends in the fifteenth century would have encouraged special council of advisers. The advisers concluded that the king was right, that Columbus's ideas were founded upon imagination, not fact.

Columbus had failed on two counts. He had not supplied believable scientific evidence to convince the learned council that his plan was feasible, and he had asked for too many rewards in return for his efforts. His reputation suffered greatly. To make matters worse, King John sent an expedition of his own men out on a trip to cross the

such a belief, and one scientific theory speculated that if the world was geometrically balanced, then there had to be a fourth continent. That is, Europe and Africa had to be balanced by Asia and an unknown continent. The Bible added proof by indicating that there was more land on the earth than water, a strong argument for Columbus's idea.

Christopher satisfied himself that he could make the trip, but he had trouble convincing others that he was right. He had sailed near the equator and interviewed people in Africa and found that one could live in tropical climates without roasting. He had studied the winds and ocean currents carefully on all his voyages, and he knew that there was a current and wind pattern to the north that would allow him to sail back to Europe. He did not believe in sea monsters, although he was not too sure about strangely deformed people living on islands in the Ocean Sea. And, because of his miscalculation of the distance to Asia, he believed that he could supply enough food and water on his ships to make the journey there.

Exactly what Christopher knew or suspected to be in the Ocean Sea is still debated by scholars. Columbus probably had in mind two things in planning his trip. One, that he would reach Asia; and two, that he would encounter unclaimed islands or mainlands on the way. It is fairly certain that he suspected that he would find unknown lands between Europe and Asia where he could, at least, resupply his ships. Every source of his knowledge told him to expect to find islands in the Ocean Sea. This belief was so strong that he insisted before kings and commissions that, if he did find continents or islands, they should be given to him to rule.

Ocean Sea shortly after rejecting Columbus's plan. To Christopher, it looked as if King John had stolen his ideas! The king's expedition failed, and Columbus felt deceived. He learned that he could never again tell all the details of his plan in public.

Christopher now decided to leave Portugal and go to Spain, a much larger and wealthier country. So in 1485, at the age of thirty-four, he left Portugal with his small son, Diego, and sailed for Palos in Spain. He had chosen to go to Palos because Felipa's sister, Diego's aunt, lived nearby in Huelva. She could look after small Diego while Columbus continued to seek support for his dream.

## La Rábida Monastery

La Rábida and the nearby port town of Palos are important places in the life of Christopher Columbus. The whitewashed monastery is located on a hill, surrounded by trees and gardens, overlooking the Tinto River on one side and the Atlantic Ocean on the other. The full name of the monastery is Santa Maria de La Rábida.

Originally, the site was a Moslem fortress that was converted into a Franciscan monastery in the thirteenth century. By the fifteenth century, it was well-known as a center for scientific learning. The balconies were used as observatories to study the stars, and the library of the monastery was one of the largest in Spain. It probably had a primary school for boys, which the young Diego may have attended.

Basically, of course, the monastery was a religious house where the Franciscans studied and worshiped God. They were involved in sending missionaries to the coasts of Africa and out to Atlantic islands such as the Canary Islands and the Madeira Islands, where Columbus had lived.

At the monastery, Columbus had the opportunity to talk to a number of learned Franciscans and leading men from the town of Palos. There he could discuss his plans with people who knew the sea, knew about geography and other sciences. He could walk in the gardens and think about his plans and refine them. He could use the library to learn more about the earth.

In 1837, the monastery was closed by the government of Spain, and

But Christopher did not go immediately to Huelva when he and Diego landed at Palos. Instead, he spent several weeks at the nearby Franciscan church and monastery named La Rábida. People have wondered why he did this, since La Rábida was somewhat out of his way. The answer probably is related to Columbus's religious nature. He always celebrated Mass after a voyage, and he had met Franciscan friars while living in Madeira who were under the supervision of La Rábida. He may also have heard that La Rábida was a monastery with a good library and that the friars there were interested in science.

\* \* \*

people plundered the many artifacts, books, plants, and works of art in the buildings. Today, La Rábida is no longer a monastery, but a few Franciscans keep it open for tourists who wish to see the rooms in which Columbus and Diego lived and worked.

*This nineteenth-century painting is the artist Eugène Delacroix's conception of Christopher and Diego after they have arrived at La Rábida after their long journey from Portugal. While the young Diego rests, Christopher is captivated by the large map on the wall.*

Whatever reason led him to La Rábida, it was one of the most important events in his life. There he met Friar Antonio de Marchena. Friar Marchena was a highly respected churchman who had served Queen Isabella, and he was a cosmographer (one who studies the structure of the universe in all its parts: cosmography includes geology, geography, and astronomy) and a good astrologer. (In those days, astronomers were called astrologers.)

Better still, Christopher and Friar Marchena became immediate friends. Columbus finally had found a confidant, someone whom he could trust, to whom he could tell his entire plan in detail, who saw the merit of the plan, who could help him collect scientific data and detail, and someone with the right political connections to help him convince the king and queen to support his journey.

The two men talked for days and long into many nights. Christopher told him everything—his life story, his adventures at sea, and his many theories about sailing across the Ocean Sea. Friar Marchena was a friend who kept his secrets. Columbus would say later, "I never got anything from anyone, except Friar Antonio de Marchena, that is besides what was given to me by the eternal God."

These discussions were good for Christopher. He had someone with scientific knowledge who could question each point of his plan. And he had a friend who could help him find the supporting scientific and religious documents needed to promote his idea. The religious documentation was important because, in the fifteenth century, the Bible was considered the primary authority for any aspect of knowledge.

Until then, Columbus had had a strong belief that sailing across the Ocean Sea was possible, based on his years of experience as a seaman. Later, he would claim that the idea had been planted in his mind by God. As a sailor, he had studied the winds and currents, he knew about the foreign objects that had been found washed up on island shores, and he had heard the tales of old sailors. Further, he had experimented with sailing the tropical waters to see if one could survive in the hotter zones of the earth. What he lacked was scientific theory and biblical indications that the trip was possible. Friar Marchena impressed on him the necessity for reading as much as he could about the Ocean Sea and Asia in order to defend his ideas before possible supporters.

Friar Marchena was so impressed with his new friend that he used his influence with important people to help bring Christopher's ideas to the attention of those people who had the riches to support Christopher's enterprise.

First Friar Marchena sent Christopher to see two of the wealthiest dukes in Spain. Both were interested and wanted to support him with ships and crews, but because of political events, they were unable to do so. The Duke Medina Celi contacted the queen in order to get her blessing for such an undertaking. It turned out that she was interested in the project herself.

Unfortunately, King Ferdinand and Queen Isabella were at war against the province of Granada, which was the last stronghold of the Moslems (called Moors) in Spain. Much of Spain had been captured by Moslem invaders in the early eighth century, making Spain a part of the great Islamic Empire that stretched from modern-day Iran to the Ocean Sea, including North Africa and Spain. These Arab invaders had been stopped at the French border by several medieval kings, most importantly, King Charlemagne. Thus, much of Spain had belonged to the Islamic Empire for almost eight hundred years. King Ferdinand and Queen Isabella were determined to drive the Moslems from their country.

Christopher located the king and queen at their headquarters near Madrid in January 1486. He was allowed to present his ideas and plans to the monarchs. Because of Friar Marchena, he had now developed a scientific and religious case for his project, making him better prepared than he had been with King John II in Portugal. He brought along a map of the world that he and his brother Bartholomew had drawn. As he presented his plans, he quoted from the Bible and famous ancient books that supported his theories.

# Controversial Maps
# Associated with Columbus

Could Columbus have seen older maps and charts that showed the American continent? Scholars have long argued that this is possible. Two of the most frequently noted maps are the so-called Vineland Map and the map of the Italian humanist Toscanelli.

The Vineland map was discovered and published by Yale University in 1965. It created a lot of excitement at the time because it shows in its western section, the Atlantic northwest, geographical features of North America. The map was supposedly drawn in 1440, almost fifty years before Columbus sailed, and was copied from a much earlier map. Paper analysis and historical evidence, however, have shown this map to be a fake and probably drawn in the twentieth century.

Paolo del Pozzo Toscanelli and his chart are another matter. Toscanelli was a noted Renaissance geographer and scientist who lived in Florence, Italy. He had supplied geographical information to the Portuguese king with a map showing the Ocean Sea. Columbus read this information while in Portugal and was excited about it.

*People were very excited when the so-called Vineland map was found. It is supposed to show the area of Vineland discovered by the Viking explorer Leif Ericson. Notice the land off Greenland in the upper left. Chemical analysis of the paper and ink, however, has proved this map to be a clever forgery.*

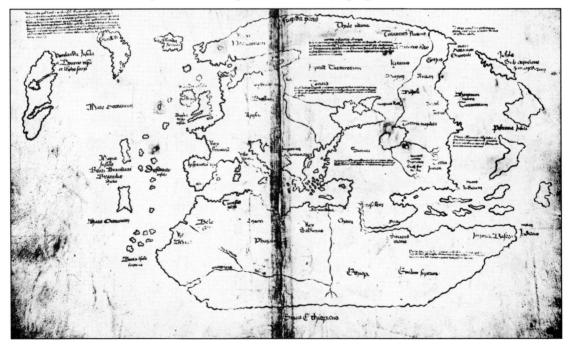

Scholars continue to disagree, however, as to whether Columbus and Toscanelli then corresponded or whether Columbus simply used the information sent to the Portuguese king. Two important geographic ideas of Toscanelli influenced Columbus. First, Toscanelli estimated the distance from Portugal to Asia as being 130 degrees, with each degree representing approximately 56⅔ miles (the exact distance that Toscanelli had in mind is in question). The measure of the degree is used, since the world is round. A circle has 360 degrees. Therefore, all one had to do was know the length of a degree, at the equator, in order to calculate how far it was around the globe. Second, Toscanelli's map, which does not survive, was probably drawn from the new linear perspective being used in Florence. In that city, artists and others looked at objects, whether they were an apple or the entire world, through a grid of lines. By placing a real or imagined grid of crossed lines in front of any object, it could be drawn in proportion to everything else surrounding it. In the case of the Ocean Sea, one imagined standing above the ocean, in space, looking down. Then the ocean could be drawn in relation to the rest of the world. This made the Ocean Sea appear less threatening, more like a real place, similar to the rest of the known world. Crossing it became a simple matter of moving from degree to degree; that is, it could be taken one step at a time.

*The Toscanelli map (reconstructed by Bjorn Landstrom in Columbus, New York, 1967). The map drawn by Toscanelli that Columbus probably used has not survived. This drawing represents what that map may have looked like, based on a letter written by Toscanelli to the king of Portugal. The important thing about Toscanelli's map is that it is drawn with a grid. By using a grid, Europe, the Ocean Sea, and Asia take on a spacial relationship to one another. The Ocean Sea is less frightening because it can be taken a step (or grid) at a time.*

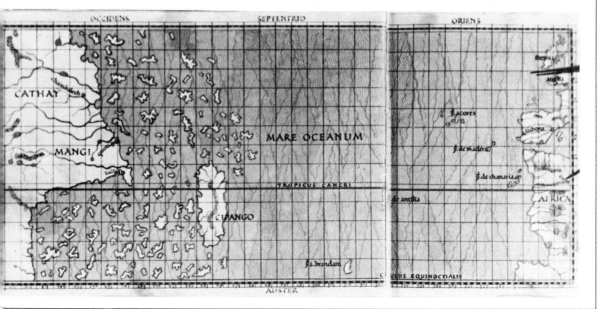

# What Did Columbus Study?

Historians know almost nothing about the education of Christopher Columbus. He may have attended the primary school run by the cloth merchants in Genoa, as indicated in Chapter One. There is no record of this, however. When he arrived in Lisbon, he began making maps and charts with his brother Bartholomew, but no one knows where the two brothers learned this skill. Both seemed to begin to read and write while in Lisbon in business as mapmakers.

Christopher spoke the Genoese dialect of Italian, but he could not write it. He probably could read and write some in Latin. Christopher and Bartholomew learned to read and write in Spanish, even though they were living in Portugal, because Spanish was considered the most important language to know during the fifteenth century.

As Columbus developed his scientific arguments to support his dream, he read many important books. His favorite was a book entitled *Imago mundi,* or *Image of the World,* by a French churchman by the name of Pierre D'Ailly. The *Imago mundi* was filled with facts about the world, astronomy, and geography. Columbus filled the margins of his copy of the book with his own notations. He also liked a world historical geography written by an Italian named Enea Silvio Piccolomini, who became Pope Pius II. Through these two books, he was introduced to the ideas of many ancient and medieval thinkers and what they believed about the Ocean Sea.

Christopher also studied travel literature by people who had either been to the Far East, or else pretended that they had. He was influenced by Sir John Mandeville, who wrote the most popular travel guide in the late Middle Ages. Sir John presented an exotic Asia where luxuries abounded. He strongly advocated that one could get to Asia by sailing across the Ocean Sea. Although it is doubtful that Sir John Mandeville ever traveled to Asia (in fact, we do not even know who this mysterious writer might have been), his ideas fit and supported Columbus's beliefs.

Christopher later bought a copy of Marco Polo's *Travels.* Marco Polo had traveled overland to China during the thirteenth century and wrote a book about that country. Besides these books, Columbus always read his Bible. He loved Bible stories, and he was especially interested in what the Bible said about the earth, its size, shape, and how much land and water was on the earth. He was very much interested in the "lost gold mines" of King Solomon of the Old Testament, and in biblical prophecies that told of unknown islands in the seas.

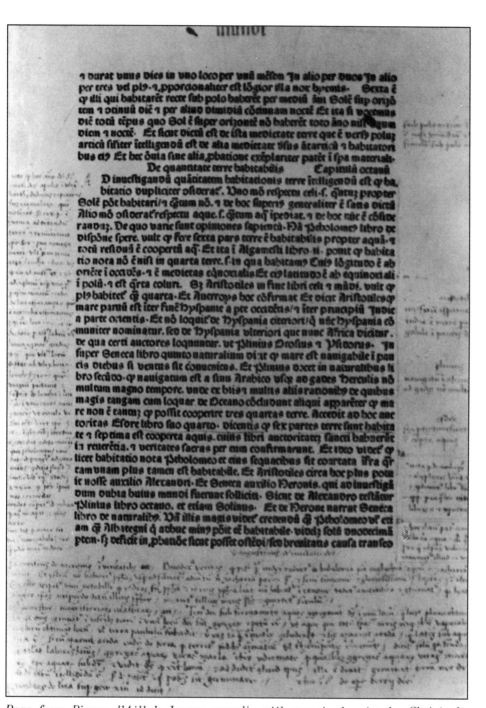

Page from Pierre d'Ailly's Imago mundi, *with marginal notes by Christopher* Columbus. *The* Imago mundi *was one of Columbus's favorite books, and the copy he used survives for us to study today. Pierre d'Ailly summarized everything known in the fifteenth century about geography and related information. Christopher made 898 marginal notes on the pages of this book.*

# The Voyage of St. Brandan

Were there earlier voyages from Europe that found the Americas? The answer to this question is yes. It is certain that the Vikings landed on the coasts of what is today Canada. Earlier discoveries, however, are only guesses based on strong legends and myths. One of the most interesting is the legend of St. Brandan, an Irish monk from the sixth century. According to the story, Brandan and fourteen fellow monks sailed from Galway, Ireland, in a little boat made from ox hides. After forty days, they landed on an island where they were well received, housed, and fed. Then for the next eight years, they sailed from island to island witnessing many marvels. No one knows if this is based on a true event or not. But there are many such tales of Europeans sailing out into the Ocean Sea and discovering islands that might have been the very ones discovered later by Columbus. Even in the New World itself there are legends, such as the Quetzalcoatl myth of the Aztec Indians, which would seem to indicate visits by earlier explorers. Quetzalcoatl was described as a blond-haired, fair-skinned visitor who promised to return one day. The Aztecs believed Quetzalcoatl to be a god.

*St. Brandan and his monks at sea (Bodleian Library, Oxford, England)*

But he still did not convince the king and queen. A journey across the Ocean Sea would be expensive, and Spain needed all the money in the treasury for the war against the Moslems.

Ferdinand and Isabella did not turn him down completely, however. Friar Marchena pleaded with them to consider the proposal seriously, and in the end they, like King John II of Portugal before them, turned the issue over to a council of advisers composed of churchmen and scientists. But the council did not get around to discussing Columbus's ideas until late in 1486 and early in 1487. In the meantime, Columbus followed the monarchs as they traveled from town to town.

In the fifteenth century, there was no permanent capital for the king and queen and their court. Instead, they traveled from province to province and from nobleman's castle to nobleman's castle, staying at each place for several weeks, holding court and doing the business of government. Each place they stayed had to finance their stay with housing and food. This could become very expensive, so the court did not stay too long in any one place.

## The Viking Discoveries

About A.D. 1000, Leif Ericson established a Viking colony on "Vineland" to the west of Greenland. Both Viking sagas and archaeological evidence confirm the presence of Vikings in what is today Newfoundland. At a site named L'Anse aux Meadows, archaeologists have found the remains of a village with nine buildings and a smithy. Viking sagas tell of expeditions of ships sailing to the coast of what is now North America to cut trees for lumber for their colonies in Greenland and Iceland. Much has been made of these early discoveries, and debates are frequent in which some supporters of the Vikings feel they should get the credit for discovery rather than Columbus. The difference is that the Vikings did nothing with their discovery. Columbus spread the word about the new lands and immediately returned with colonists. Earlier, in the eleventh century, Europe was not ready to explore and settle such far-off places, and the Vikings never informed the rest of Europe about the newfound lands.

*This family portrait was done by a Spanish artist long after all the persons in the picture were dead. It is intended to show Christopher, Beatriz Enríquez de Harana, Diego, and Ferdinand discussing geography as they study the globe, a map, and a sailing chart. Beatriz is bringing them fruit for a snack.*

The months Christopher spent following the court throughout Spain were beneficial in the end. The king, the queen, and other officials got to know him better. Some scoffed at his ideas, but others listened, and he made important friends at the court. As he traveled, he studied, reading more books and looking at ocean charts to perfect his plan.

While the royal court was staying at Cordova, he met the lovely Beatriz Enríquez de Harana and fell in love with her. He was thirty-seven years old; she was twenty. He never married her, but she bore his second son, Ferdinand, in 1488. Ferdinand would be devoted to his father and would write a famous biography of him, one of our chief sources of information about the admiral.

We know very little about Beatriz. She was a daughter of humble peasants from a mountain village near Cordova. Christopher rarely mentioned her in his writings, and Ferdinand, their son, never wrote about her at all. Christopher loved her, however, and provided for her support, and in his will he left her adequate income following his death.

Most likely Columbus did not marry Beatriz, because it would have been against the law once he received his titles after the first voyage to the New World. In fifteenth-century Spain, the king and queen did not allow people with noble titles to marry commoners. Why he did not marry her earlier, we do not know.

Columbus was able to follow the king and queen around Spain because they put him on the royal payroll while waiting for a decision from their council of advisers concerning his plan to sail across the Ocean Sea. Outside of his continued studies, we have almost no information about what he did during these months, except references to the fact that he frequently talked to everyone about his plans to the point of boring some of the regular members of the royal court.

*Columbus arguing his idea that one could sail west in order to arrive in Asia. He was well prepared as he met learned councils. He brought with him maps, quotations from books, and mathematical calculations to prove his points. Here is an artist's rendering of how he might have looked before those councils of scholars.*

# Geographic Knowledge in the Fifteenth Century

Cosmography and geography in the fifteenth century often sound like fairy tales to us today. Many believed the world to consist of one large land mass divided into Europe, Asia, and Africa, surrounded by water. The large ocean was supposed to contain some unknown islands, but these were inhabited by strange creatures, such as men with one eye in the center of their forehead or men with three legs. Some believed that on one unknown island lived a whole population of women only. These women were the Amazons, who had amazing strength and were very beautiful. Such fanciful thinking is not unlike our own today when we try to visualize what beings from other planets might look like.

*This map is typical of those drawn during the Middle Ages. It is called a T-O map because of its shape. The O is the flat circular disk surrounded by water. The downstroke, or stem of the T, is the Mediterranean Sea. The cross stroke, or top of the T, are the Don and Nile rivers. The T divides the world into the three known continents: Europe on the bottom left, Africa on the bottom right, and Asia on the top.*

This map is from an anonymous manuscript drawn during the thirteenth century. The map is a more elaborate form of the T-O map. It is concerned more with spiritual rather than physical geography as evidenced by the large picture of Christ above and dragons below. The two places that were of most concern to medieval mapmakers were the locations of Jerusalem (at the center of the world), and the Garden of Eden (shown here by pictures of Adam and Eve). The map is drawn with east to the top. The wall to the top left is not the wall of China; rather, it represents the wall behind which Alexander the Great supposedly imprisoned the hordes of Gog and Magog, the figures from the Biblical book of Revelations.

Even the single continent had unknown regions, and men speculated about who lived in them. Many believed that somewhere was the magical kingdom of Prester John. Prester John was a mythical Christian king who had fled Europe with his people and had established a godly kingdom somewhere in Africa or Asia. It was also believed that somewhere was the original Garden of Eden from which Adam and Eve had been driven.

Everyone knew that the world was round, but many questioned whether one could sail around it. If the world consisted of one large land mass surrounded by ocean, then it had to be a long way from the western shore to the eastern shore. Maps were not very good during the Middle Ages, and they were just beginning to improve during Columbus's lifetime. Since almost no one had been across the Ocean Sea, except for a few who had not told their story to the scholars, it was a place of complete mystery.

*This Ptolemy map was drawn in 1477. Ptolemy was a geographer who lived in the Egyptian city of Alexandria during the second century. He wrote a famous book containing all that was known about the world, and then gave instructions on how to draw the world. The cartographer in 1477 faithfully followed Ptolemy's directions to produce this map. Notice that Africa is mostly an unknown continent below the Sahara Desert, and that the Indian Ocean (*Mare Indicum*) was believed to be an enclosed sea.*

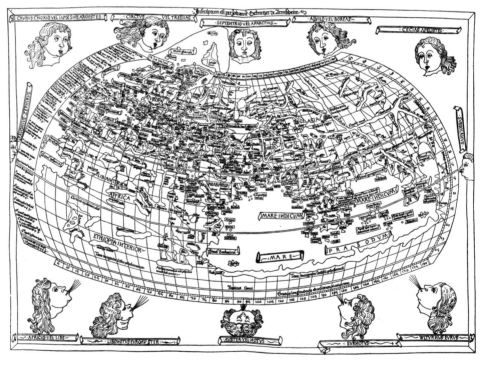

Finally, the council of advisers submitted their recommendations to the king and queen. They rejected Christopher's ideas as impossible and ill-founded! They were especially concerned with how he calculated the distance to Asia. The council, using sources different from Columbus's, calculated the distance to be at least four times as far as the 2,500 miles Christopher had figured. Thus, it was impossible to reach Asia by sea. No ship could carry enough supplies to last the many months such a long journey would require. The council's advice to the monarchs was to deny Columbus their support.

Christopher was crushed! After months of trying to sell his idea to the Spanish king and queen, he was now turned down. He was taken off the royal payroll in June 1488. In the meantime, Christopher's brother Bartholomew had once again sought support for him from King John II of Portugal, to be turned down a second time.

## Asian Discoveries of the New World

Just as there are many myths and legends about European sailors crossing the Atlantic Ocean to the New World before Columbus, so there are also many myths and legends about Asians crossing the Pacific Ocean. Obviously, the first settlers came from Asia across the Bering Strait as early as twenty-five thousand to thirty thousand years ago, as they were the forerunners of Native Americans.

There are stories as well about Buddhist monks who sailed across the north Pacific and down the Pacific coast of America as far as Mexico in the fifth century A.D. Other stories tell of a fleet sent out by the famous Asian ruler Kublai Khan. The fleet was thrown off course by a storm, and the survivors told of a strange land to the east. Many have used the theory of cultural diffusion to show earlier voyages from Asia. According to this theory, migrations of peoples can be traced by comparing common cultural traits of groups living great distances apart. For instance, there is a remarkable similarity in such things as the style of pottery and religious images between the Chinese and natives of Mexico and South America.

The future discoverer of the New World did not give up easily, however. He had complete faith in himself and in his plan. He returned to the court and again tried for several months to interest the king and queen in his enterprise, without success.

In February 1488, Bartholomew went to England to try to convince King Henry VII to support the journey. Although no documents survive in England relating to this visit, we know that Bartholomew presented King Henry VII with a world map to show the possibility that Asia could be reached by sailing west.

Queen Isabella, however, had not been totally convinced by her advisers to reject Christopher's ideas. She knew that once the Moors were driven from Spain, her country would have to establish better trade routes to the east. Europeans wanted goods that could be had only from Asia, especially spices for their foods. Portugal was actively seeking a trade route to Asia by trying to round the southern tip of Africa. If Portugal succeeded in establishing a water route to Asia, then it would become a much stronger nation than Spain because of the increased revenue such trade would produce. Spain would have to find another route or a better route because Portugal would protect her shipping lane around Africa and not allow other country to benefit from it. Isabella was also very interested in sending missionaries to Asia to teach the Christian faith.

Columbus's arguments appealed to her. She saw in him a potential for success the others discounted. So even though she and her husband, the king, had turned down his request for support, she gave Christopher a small gift of money in June 1488, to enable him to continue his efforts.

Christopher returned to La Rábida and started to plan negotiations with the king of France. Friar Marchena, his friend and confidant, talked him into staying in Spain and encouraged him to be patient. Christopher tried to interest several wealthy noblemen in his enterprise, and although many were enthusiastic about his plans, none would pay for it. One duke, Don Luis de la Cerda Medinaceli, went so far as to begin paying Columbus a small wage and to authorize planning for ships to be ordered for the enterprise. This duke encouraged the king and queen to reconsider their rejection of Christopher's plan. He believed that the project was extremely important to the future of Spain.

Don Luis's encouragement caused Queen Isabella to take fresh interest in Columbus's plan. She wrote to Christopher and asked that he return to court again to discuss his ideas with her and her councillors. During in the summer of 1489, many of Columbus's important acquaintances began to promote his plans to the queen. They included Cardinal Mendoza, the highest-ranking churchman in Spain, Father Diego Deza, the tutor of Prince Juan, heir to the throne, and Alfonso de Quintanilla, the court treasurer.

That summer, Christopher finally seems to have convinced the queen that Spain should finance his journey. She wanted him to wait for final confirmation until the war was over. Even that looked promising as the Spanish troops enjoyed victory after victory.

Then the war bogged down. Weeks turned into months and months into years. Some biographers have held that Columbus actually fought in some of the battles as he waited. Columbus followed the court for a while and then accepted the hospitality of Don Luis to stay at his house for several weeks. Then he returned to La Rábida. Everyone told him to be patient.

At La Rábida, he met Friar John Perez, who had been Queen Isabella's confessor. The two became friends immediately, and, along with Friar Marchena, Friar Perez became one of his best friends.

Noticing how poor Columbus was and that he was becoming impatient with Queen Isabella's lack of action, Friar Perez went to the royal court in 1491 to talk to the queen about the project. Christopher was once again planning to go to France to try to sell his idea to the French king. The queen sent him a gift of money and asked him to return to court again. In December 1491, Christopher, accompanied by Friar Perez, returned to the royal court. The war ended just before they arrived, and Columbus watched as the king and queen entered the great Moslem stronghold city of Granada.

It was a time of great festivity. The Moslem rule in Spain was over in January 1492, after nearly eight hundred years! Some of the most

*Christopher and young Diego at La Rábida monastery. In this enamel painting, the artist depicts Christopher explaining his "enterprise of the Indies" to Friar John Perez while Diego is comforted by another monk.*

important people in Spain had come to witness the surrender. The queen decided to take up the issue of Columbus's enterprise once more. She had her pick of advisers because the city was filled with churchmen, noblemen, cosmographers, astrologers, and philosophers. Now Christopher had many friends among the monarchs' advisers who were appointed to a new council to consider his proposal.

The advisers were divided in their opinions about the potential success of the enterprise. The debate lasted for days, and Columbus was optimistic. In the end, however, the council could not bring itself to advise the queen to support Columbus. The problem was that he had again asked for too much reward for himself.

Columbus insisted that if he were successful, the king and queen should grant him the titles, Admiral of the Ocean Sea, Viceroy, and Governor over all the lands he discovered. Furthermore, these titles were to be held by his family forever. He also insisted upon unusually high financial rewards if he were successful. He wanted 10 percent of all the profits that might result from his discoveries. The council advised the queen once more to turn him down.

Christopher left court immediately. He was angry, frustrated, hurt, and discouraged. He decided to go back to La Rábida and then on to France, the one country to which he had not yet appealed.

But Columbus's friends at court had not given up. They continued to argue his case, for many of them had the foresight to understand what his enterprise could mean to Spain. In an unusual turn of events, it was now King Ferdinand who took the lead in reconsidering Columbus's project. He knew that the "keeper of the privy purse," Luis de Santangel, was especially interested in Christopher's adventure, and so the king asked this official to investigate ways in which it might be financed.

Luis de Santangel was a wealthy businessman who had been called to court to manage the monarch's household moneys. He was a shrewd international dealer who knew that Spain had to compete with Portugal and the Italian city-states if the country's economy was to grow. He firmly believed that Christopher Columbus offered the best, the fastest, and the cheapest possibility for Spain to advance economically in the fifteenth century.

Almost before Columbus rode out of town on his mule (an animal the monarchs had loaned him to come to Granada), Luis de Santangel spoke to the queen, advising her that she had made a mistake. His arguments undoubtedly centered on Spanish economic rivalry with Portugal. This country, next to Spain, had been sending out expeditions, and it had been very successful. Portugal had found the passage around Africa and now could trade directly with India. Columbus might get support from another nation. After all, the man wanted only

# King Ferdinand and Queen Isabella

King Ferdinand of Aragon and Queen Isabella of Castile are two of the more fascinating rulers in the fifteenth century. They ruled as husband and wife and as co-equal monarchs. They combined their two lands in 1469 through marriage, contract, and through mutual respect for each other. Spain was not a united country in the fifteenth century, but through this marriage and alliance, its two largest regions were joined. Because of their Christian piety and love of the Church, they are known to history as the Catholic Sovereigns. Their desire was to unify all of Spain under their monarchy, creating a large and significant nation. First they had to drive the Moors from southern Spain, and then they could bring other independent parts of the territory under their control. Ferdinand's goal was to make the unified territory an important nation through diplomacy with other countries. He was not an outgoing person, or even very likable, but even though he was never an ardent supporter of Christopher like his wife, Isabella, he was the one who in the end caused a way to be found to finance the adventure.

Queen Isabella was his opposite. She was gracious, tactful, very religious, and one of the best rulers in Europe. Because of her religious fervor, she shared her husband's desire to rid Spain of the Moors, and both worked to exile the Jews as well. They wanted to make Spain totally Catholic and were intolerant of any other beliefs.

From all the sources, it is clear that Isabella and Columbus were friends from their very first meeting. They seemed to understand each other immediately: Both were religious; both were adventurous. Isabella liked the sea captain, and she had complete confidence in him. She was excited by his plans to cross the Ocean Sea, not only for the fame and fortune that would come to Spain, but more importantly for the opportunity to carry the Chris-

three ships and crews. Financing such an expedition would bring glory, power, prestige, and wealth to Spain if it was successful! And what could Spain lose? Only three ships.

These new arguments, none of them scientific, excited the imagination of the queen and the king. Luis de Santangel even had a way to pay for the journey without actually putting up too much money. The tian faith to new peoples. Queen Isabella was a sincere and pious woman who believed strongly that part of her role as queen was to encourage the salvation of souls.

One of the persistent myths about Isabella and Columbus is that she pawned her jewels in order to finance the voyage. This was never considered. Even if she had wanted to do this, she would not have been able to do so because she had already pawned her jewels to fight the war against the Moors.

*Statues of King Ferdinand and Queen Isabella from the Sacristy of the Royal Chapel, Granada Cathedral, Spain*

city of Palos had been fined and owed the king and queen two out-fitted caravels for them to use in any way they wanted.

Now was the time to collect the fine. As for the rest, investors, including Columbus, would raise the necessary money. All the problems seemed solved. The king liked the plan; the queen had always liked the idea.

Christopher had not gotten four miles out of town before a messenger on horseback overtook him and ordered him back to court. Columbus returned in triumph! Just hours before, he had left the city discouraged, and now the dream for which he had fought all those years was to be supported by the king and queen of Spain. There would be other problems, but they were all minor as far as Columbus was concerned. Now he would realize his great adventure.

Things moved much faster now. There was a new attitude of excitement at the court. Once the monarchs had committed themselves to Christopher's dream, everyone seemed willing to help. The proper documents and contracts were drawn up by the royal scribes, signed by the king and queen and by Columbus. Christopher was given funds by the monarch and by private investors. Most important, he was given letters to take to the city of Palos commanding that city to furnish two caravels for him. He arrived at Palos on May 22, 1492.

The very next day, in the beautiful little brick church of St. George, Columbus assembled the mayor, the town council of Palos, and all interested citizens. He read to them the letter from the king and queen commanding the town to supply him with two ships fully equipped and manned. The third ship, the *Santa María*, he chartered himself.

The citizens of Palos did not take these orders well. In the first place, many considered Columbus crazy, and even worse, he was a foreigner! There was no enthusiasm for his adventure in this port of sailors long accustomed to sailing up and down the African coast. To them, Christopher was a crazy Italian whom they taunted in public for suggesting such a stupid idea. No one volunteered to sail with him across the Ocean Sea.

Again, Friar Marchena came to his rescue. Friar Marchena was well known to the people of Palos as a pious man from the nearby monastery. He was a close friend of many of the sea captains and sailors in town. The most famous and respected of the captains in Palos was Martín Alonso Pinzón, and it was to him that Friar Marchena now appealed to support Columbus.

A meeting between Pinzón and Columbus was arranged, and Christopher outlined his total plan to Pinzón. Pinzón analyzed Christopher's data and plans, and he realized that they were workable from a practical point of view. Here were two excellent sea captains talking the language of seamen. They understood each other. Martín Alonso Pinzón was sold on Columbus's ideas. He came away from the meeting believing in Columbus's enterprise. With Pinzón signed on, other sailors were easier to recruit.

In the weeks that followed, sailors were signed on, supplies were gathered and stored aboard the three ships, and the ships were inspected and repaired as needed. By August 2, 1492, everything was ready. They would sail the next day.

# CHAPTER THREE

# The Great Adventure

The evening before, the sailors made their confessions to the local priest, took communion at the church of St. George in Palos, and went aboard ship. Before dawn, Christopher made his confession to Friar John Perez, his friend and supporter, took communion, and then was rowed out to his flagship, the *Santa María*. As dawn's light began to break and as the tide began to turn, the three small ships—the *Pinta*, the *Niña*, and the *Santa María*—made their way down the Saltes River to the open sea. Columbus was on his way at last!

Actually, we know a lot about the voyage of discovery because Christopher Columbus did an unusual thing. He kept a diary, or log, of his journey. Although keeping a detailed ship's log became normal in the following years, Columbus was one of the first to do so, and his is one of the best.

Unfortunately, we no longer have the original diary that he wrote. A copy was made of it before it disappeared, and that copy was used by the bishop Bartolomé de las Casas, who wrote one of the earliest biographies of Columbus. This copy of Christopher's original log has been lost too. Bartolomé de las Casas made his own copy of the copy,

*Theodore de Bry published the first "picture book" of the New World in 1594 using the technique of woodcuts. (Woodcuts are blocks of wood carved by artists which could be inked and pressed on paper to produce multiple copies of a picture.) He illustrated many of the events in the life of Christopher Columbus and tried to show the people and flora and fauna of the New World to Europeans. He had not traveled there, however, and he had to rely on reports of others. In this woodcut, de Bry shows a fanciful picture of Columbus saying goodbye to King Ferdinand and Queen Isabella as he left Palos on the first voyage. As we know, neither Ferdinand nor Isabella was there to see him off.*

summarizing many parts. He had complained that the copy he had used had numerous inaccuracies, but Las Casas's summary covers much of the trip, and we will, in this chapter, quote from Robert Fuson's translation of that log (see bibliography) to let Columbus tell much of his adventure in his own words.

The first day was uneventful. By evening they had covered nearly sixty miles and set their course for the Canary Islands. At dark, they lit lanterns so that the ships would not lose sight of one another, and soon after nightfall the sailors gathered on deck to sing the "Salve Regina" and to offer evening prayers. Night watch began soon after. All night long, it was the responsibility of the "ship's boy" to watch the hourglass, turn it when the sand ran out, and call out the hours as they passed.

On the fourth day out, the *Pinta*'s rudder broke, and several hours were lost in making repairs. The repairs held only one day, and the rudder broke again. On top of that, the *Pinta* began to leak. Grand Canary Island was finally sighted on August 8, where the *Pinta* could either be traded for another ship or repaired. As it turned out, there were no other ships at any of the Canary Islands, so the *Pinta* had to be docked, the rudder repaired, and the seams recaulked to stop the leaking. At the same time, the sails on the *Niña* were changed from triangular "lateen" sails to square riggings like the other two ships.

Columbus explains:

*I have determined that the most efficient action is to make a new rudder for the Pinta. Also, I have determined that the Niña should be square-rigged as the other ships and have ordered the lateen sails altered. This will enable the Niña to follow the other ships more closely and safely in the belt of the easterlies. These winds blow steadily from the east or NE every day of the year and a square-rigged ship has every advantage in these latitudes.*

Considerable time had been lost. By September 6, everything was again ready, the ships were repaired, new provisions of firewood and water were taken aboard, and the sailors made their confessions and took communion at the church of San Sebastian. As they prepared to sail from the harbor, word arrived that Portuguese ships were only a few hours away with orders to capture Christopher and take him to Lisbon. King John II was taking no chances. He did not believe

# The Diary, or Ship's Log, of Columbus

A ship's log is the daily record of activities aboard a ship. In 1492, keeping such a record was just becoming popular among ships' captains, but most of them are very brief, giving the reader little more than locations, wind directions, ship's speed, and weather conditions. Christopher went beyond that to record as much as he could about his adventure. Some passages are very long, where he described what he saw or commented on events. It is a very valuable document for historians and others interested in the discovery.

Unfortunately, the original log is lost. The copy Columbus made while still aboard ship he gave to Queen Isabella at Barcelona when he returned. She had a scribe make an exact copy of it for Christopher, which was given to him at Cadiz just before he sailed on the second voyage to the new world. That copy is lost also, but there is record of it as late as 1554.

Most of Christopher Columbus's personal papers, books, maps, and letters were put in the hands of his son Ferdinand for safekeeping. Ferdinand was a collector of books and had one of the largest personal libraries in the sixteenth century. After Ferdinand died, his library, including all the materials owned by his father, eventually was given to the cathedral at Seville. The fathers at the cathedral did not take care of the library, and about 75 percent of it was destroyed or lost.

Christopher's grandson, Luis Columbus, was the black sheep of the family. He was continually in trouble and in need of money. He sold off parts of his grandfather's materials to get extra money. In 1554, he sold the scribe's copy of the log to a printer. It was never printed, and after that sale, it has never again been seen.

As noted above, we are lucky that it was used by the first bishop in the

Christopher could really reach Asia, but he was not going to let him try either. Christopher was worried. The wind died down, and Columbus's small fleet made little progress, but then neither did the Portuguese.

New World, Bartolome de las Casas, before it was lost. Las Casas wrote one of the earliest biographies of Christopher Columbus (as a part of a larger history of the Indies) and had free access to all the Columbus family papers to do so. In the course of preparing his history, Las Casas made an abstract of the log for his own use, which he titled "The Book of the First Voyage." This is the only source of the log we have today. Sometimes the bishop would summarize the log, and at other times he would copy it exactly. He was careful to copy exactly the sections that told of Columbus's trip through the Caribbean Islands.

So how good is our source for the first voyage? The Las Casas copy is probably fairly accurate, as the bishop was an honest man. He was also a scholar who was careful to get his facts right. He had been to many of the places mentioned in the log when later he was bishop at Hispaniola in the New World. It is probable, however, that there are errors. Las Casas himself complained that the scribe who copied the original made mistakes. Scholars who have studied the log through the years feel that most of the mistakes are in directions and other technical details.

Another source for the log is the biography of Christopher's son Ferdinand. He too used the scribe's copy of the log in his book. Unfortunately, Ferdinand's original biography is lost also. All we have is a very poor Italian translation of Ferdinand's original, which he wrote in Spanish. But sometimes the only entry we have for a particular event is found in Ferdinand's biography.

Scholars have to consider the origins of their source material carefully. Just because a document is old or written by someone close to the event does not necessarily mean that the document can be used without careful criticism. The log of Christopher Columbus is an invaluable source document for our knowledge of the voyage of discovery, but it also has flaws and errors of which the reader must be aware.

Finally at 3:00 A.M. on Saturday, September 8, the northeast wind began to blow, and Columbus's ships began to move. By Sunday they were completely out of sight of any land, and the small fleet picked up speed.

# The Ships of Columbus
# and Their Technology

As strange as it may seem, we have no record of what Columbus's three ships looked like. There are no written descriptions and no paintings depicting the three ships. The pictures shown here are models based on the best available information; but even so, all we have are models that are based on ships of approximately the same kind and size as the originals. One of the more exciting research projects going on right now is by underwater archaeologists who are searching for fifteenth- and sixteenth-century wrecks of ships similar to those sailed by Columbus. By finding even a few beams of ancient ships, these scholars can then re-create a more accurate picture of these ships through computer modeling.

The *Santa María* was a type of ship called a nau. A nau was a small, round vessel, slow moving and used mostly for carrying cargo. The *Santa María* was not from Palos like the *Pinta* and *Niña*. She belonged to Juan de la Cosa, who rented her to Columbus. Juan went along as pilot of the *Santa María*. He is also an important figure for us because he drew a map of the Atlantic and Caribbean with its islands in 1501, based on his experiences sailing through those waters. This is the earliest surviving map we have of that area. The *Santa María* was larger than the *Pinta* and the *Niña* and had quarters aboard for Columbus. To complicate matters, the late fifteenth century was a time in which ship technology was changing rapidly. How much of this change had affected Columbus's fleet, we do not know. The *Santa María* was somewhere between 90 to 100 tons (that means that she could carry 90 to 100 barrels of wine, for each barrel weighed about a ton). She was probably 80 to 90 feet long. Christopher never liked this ship.

The *Niña* with Vicente Pinzón as captain was his favorite. She was a caravel of about 60 tons, a fast little ship about 75 feet long. When the trip began, she was equipped with lateen (triangle) sails. Columbus changed these to square sails at the Canary Islands. What other modifications he made, we do not know.

The *Pinta* has even more mystery. She was probably about the same size as the *Niña*. The *Pinta* was the fastest of the fleet and frequently went ahead of the others. She had to be held back to stay in sight of the other two. Her captain was Martín Pinzón.

The *Santa María* was wrecked off the coast of Hispaniola on the first voyage. The *Pinta* is not heard from again after the first voyage, so we have no idea what happened to her.

The *Niña* continued to sail for Columbus. It was the *Niña* that brought him home from the first voyage. He selected her for his second voyage and eventually bought a half share in her. She went back to Hispaniola in 1498, before Columbus's third voyage. Her final fate is unknown.

When compared to Columbus's first voyage across the unknown expanse of the Ocean Sea, modern explorers are much better prepared and have an extensive knowledge of what awaits them. The technology of Columbus's voyage consisted of only four instruments for guidance and Christopher's genius for dead reckoning. He had a compass, a half-hour glass, an astrolabe, and a quadrant. The compass would be mounted next to the helmsman, who checked it against the pole star.

Christopher tried to use a simple quadrant through which one could sight the stars and get a reading for latitude from a string that hung from the top. The quadrant, however, was almost impossible to use accurately aboard a rolling ship at sea. Navigating by the stars was only beginning to be used in the late fifteenth century. It could be quite accurate, but the pilots on Columbus's voyage were not familiar with it. Columbus seldom used it, but by the third and fourth voyages he had become more familiar with the system.

The method mostly used by Columbus to guide his ships across the ocean was known as dead reckoning. Using the compass to keep the course (and checking it against the pole star every night), the speed of the ship, and the time elapsed (using the half-hour glass), the ship's position could be entered on a chart showing approximately where it was. Speed was calculated by both the experience of feeling it and by crudely measuring it. Columbus recorded his speed by using Roman miles per hour and distance traveled per day in leagues. A league equaled four Roman miles. To measure his speed, he used the common method of tossing a small, especially designed log over the rail attached to a line that contained knots equally spaced. The number of knots in the line that went over the rail in a half minute gave the speed of the ship. Thus, even today, sea speed is figured in "knots." Every watch aboard the ships measured the knots at the beginning of duty, and the speed was recorded. When the knots were multiplied by time elapsed, you could determine distance traveled.

It was not a good method, and the log shows that Columbus frequently miscalculated his distances. It is a myth that Christopher tried to keep two sets of figures, one set for himself, and one set that he showed the sailors. The myth persists that the one that he showed the sailors was always a smaller distance than he really thought he had gone so that they would not panic when they got too far out to sea.

*The* Santa María, *the* Pinta, *and the* Niña *might have looked like this as they left Palos. There is no picture of the actual ships, and there is not much description of them to go on either. Columbus's favorite was the* Niña.

For the next few days, all went well. The three ships easily outran the Portuguese warships, which turned back when they realized that they could not catch up. Then, on September 15 in the early morning hours, panic seized many of the sailors. In Columbus's words, this is what happened:

*Early this morning I saw a marvelous meteorite fall into the sea 12 or 15 miles to the southwest. This was taken by some people to be a bad omen, but I calmed them by telling of the numerous occasions that I have witnessed such events. I have to confess that this is the closest that a falling star has ever come to my ship.*

The falling star was not the only frightening thing that happened that night. As the pilots adjusted their compasses to the North Star, they found that their instruments suddenly no longer recorded true north.

A compass reacts to the pull of the earth's gravity toward the North Pole. But sailors in the fifteenth century thought that it was pulled toward the North Star. Using a mark on the compass dial, they would align the instrument with the North Star before sailing. If a compass was aligned to the North Star in Europe, the compass needle would slowly move away from the setting as it traveled either east or west. The compass always indicates true magnetic north on the planet earth, not the location of the North Star. The point where a compass begins to swing from its setting is called the zone of zero declination.

Columbus and his men passed through the zone of zero declination as they crossed the Atlantic Ocean. As they did so, the needle of the compass began to swing to the left of the mark aligned to the North Star. Since navigation in the fifteenth century depended upon the North Star, to the crew it was as if their guidance system had malfunctioned. They thought that they would soon be lost in the vast ocean with no hope of return. Christopher, however, thought he had found a solution. The North Star, he said, was circling the north celestial pole while the compass stayed constant. His answer was not correct, since the compass was actually responding to the gravitation of the

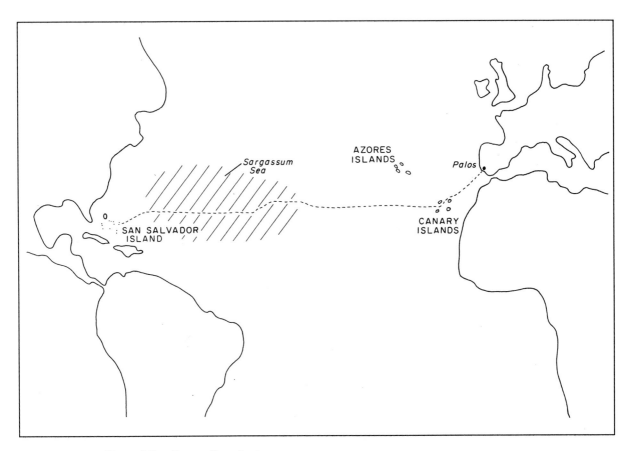

*Map of the Ocean Sea, first voyage*

North Pole on earth, but it seemed logical to those with him.

The very next day, another strange phenomenon occurred. They entered the Sargasso Sea. The sailors had never witnessed anything like the large patches of yellowish green weed floating in the water. They believed that such growth had to be attached to rocks and that the ocean must be very shallow at this point. They carefully sailed through the weed and searched for rocks and the suspected ocean bottom. Since they could not find the bottom of the ocean, they reasoned that the weed must have torn away from some distant island or reef; but the farther they sailed, the thicker it became.

Actually, sargasso is a seaweed that floats freely on small sacs filled with air attached to the leaves. It is not tied to any solid formation, nor does it break away from any Atlantic ledges or ocean banks. Columbus's log entry for Monday, September 17, describes the growth:

*I saw a great deal of weed today—weed from rocks that lie to the west. I take this to mean that we are near land. The weed resembles star-grass, except that it has long stalks and shoots and is loaded with fruit like the mastic tree. Some of this weed looks like river grass, and the crew found a live crab in a patch of it. This is a sure sign of land, for crabs are not found even 240 miles from shore. . . . We saw a lot of porpoises and the men of the Niña killed one with a harpoon. All the indications of land come from the west, where I trust Almighty God, in whose hands are all victories, will soon deliver us to land.*

The next day things got back to normal, and the trip again became routine. By September 20, the men began to see terns flying over the ships. Terns were land birds, and excitement grew. Everyone expected land to be nearby. But no land appeared. Four days later, Columbus records that the crews were becoming restless and had begun to talk about mutiny:

*I am having serious trouble with the crew, despite the signs of land. . . . The more indignant they become against me. All day long and all night long those who are awake and able to get together never cease to talk to each other in circles, complaining that they will never be able to return home. They have said that it is insanity and suicidal on their part to risk their lives following the madness of a foreigner. They have said that not only am I willing to risk my life just to become a great lord, but that I have deceived them to further my ambition. . . . I am told by a few trusted men (and these are few in number!) that if I persist in going onward, the best course of action will be to throw me into the sea some night. They will then affirm that I fell overboard while taking the position of the North Star with my quadrant. . . . I know that the men are taking these complaints to the Pinzóns and that the Pinzóns have sided with them. . . . With God's help, I shall persevere.*

The Pinzóns, who had helped Columbus convince the people of Palos that his adventure was possible, were now losing faith in the

# Who Went with Columbus?

Records do survive that enable us to know the names of most of the sailors who accompanied Columbus. Since the monarchs were paying a good part of their salaries, account records show their names and homes. Other records provide the names of those employed by Columbus and his investors, most of whom served aboard the *Santa María*. There were approximately ninety men and boys assigned to the three ships. Almost all were from Palos or nearby towns. According to the records and judging from their performance, they were able and experienced sailors. After all, they were able to survive the trip with its terrible storms.

An old myth tells us that many were criminals. This is entirely false. Only four of the ninety had any criminal record at all. Only four, besides Columbus himself, were foreigners: three Italians and one Portuguese. Only four men were not sailors but represented the monarchs or held other nonseaman jobs: One was taken as an interpreter because he spoke Hebrew and Arabic, and three were doctors, one on each ship. A few were boys, probably young teenagers who were learning to be sailors, who served as pages and cabin boys.

Organizing a seafaring expedition demanded a good deal of coordination to blend together men of different backgrounds and skills. Traditionally, there were three categories of sailors: officers, petty officers, and seamen. The entire fleet would be under the command of a captain general, in this case Christopher Columbus. He was responsible for the entire fleet of ships, the expedition, and the results of the expedition. He was the supreme commander, and his orders were the law. Each ship would have its own captain, who was in charge of everything and everyone aboard his ship. Next in command was the master who had direct charge over the seamen and all the cargo, supplies, and equipment on each ship. The master decided when the ship was ready to sail. Each ship also had a pilot who guided the ship and kept track of where the ship was. He had to know how to navigate, which meant that he had to have some knowledge of astronomy, mathematics, how to use navigational instruments, and he had to have a practical experience of the sea. He was a key person, for the entire adventure depended upon the pilot's getting the ship to its destination and returning safely.

Petty officers were usually specialists needed to make the ship and the journey run smoothly. The quartermaster, for example, took care of all the supplies and equipment on the ship, the steward managed all the food and beverages and supervised the cooking of meals, the carpenter was in charge of all repairs on board. Under the carpenter would be other petty officers such as the caulker (to fill in holes and cracks in the ship) and the cooper (to repair storage containers). The last petty officer was the barber-surgeon, who looked after the health and hygiene of the crew.

Common seamen were divided into three groups: experienced sailors who could do all the tasks necessary to make the ship run, apprentice seamen who were learning all the details of running a ship, and lastly, ship's boys who served the officers' needs, swept the decks, set mess tables, served meals, and sung religious hymns at certain times of the day. Ship's boys also stood watch with the regular sailors, and it was their duty to turn the sandglass each half hour to keep track of time. They would also have chances to learn the various duties of sailors aboard ship.

Although the seamen at Palos had believed Columbus to be crazy, and even though they nearly committed mutiny and threw him overboard on the first voyage, they came to respect and admire him greatly. Twenty-one of the original ninety sailors signed on to make other voyages of discovery with Columbus.

Interestingly, there were no soldiers or priests on the first voyage. In fact, Columbus took few weapons. The cannon on each ship was very small and was meant more for sending signals than for fighting. Later paintings show the sailors armed and patrolling the decks. This is only the imagination of the artist, and there is no basis in fact.

enterprise. Furthermore, they did not like taking orders from the Italian captain of the fleet. The very next day, Martín Pinzón, captain of the *Pinta*, thought he sighted land. Everyone rejoiced! Prayers were said; hymns were sung aboard all three ships. Everyone climbed up the riggings to look for the land. But it was a false alarm. What looked like an island was only squall clouds on the horizon. More days passed, and again the crews agitated against Christopher.

On October 7, they again thought they saw land on the horizon. Joy returned to the crews, but by nightfall they all knew that another illusion had deceived them. One small comfort appeared that evening: Many large flocks of land birds flew over the ships. So they knew that land was not too far away. What Christopher and the rest of the men did not know was that they were sailing the western Atlantic during the time in which birds from North America fly south for the winter. These migrating birds fly far out into the Atlantic on their long journey every fall. Columbus, who had read in Marco Polo's travel book that there were seven thousand islands east of Asia, believed that he was sailing through some of these islands. Therefore, the birds, in his mind, were simply flying from island to island.

Three days later, Columbus faced a showdown with his crews:

*They could stand it no longer. They grumbled and complained of the long voyage, and I reproached them for their lack of spirit, telling them that for better or worse, they had to complete the enterprise on which the Catholic Sovereigns had sent them. I cheered them on as best I could, telling them of all the honors and rewards they were about to receive. I also told the men that it was useless to complain, for I had started out to find the Indies and would continue until I had accomplished that mission, with the help of our Lord.*

Christopher's perseverance paid off. October 11 began like any other day, but the crews cheered up as many signs of land began to appear: flocks of land birds flying overhead and reeds and other green plants

## What Supplies Did Columbus Take with Him?

Again we know very little about this subject, as no documents survive that list supplies taken on the first voyage. All we know is that Christopher took enough supplies to last for one year, which was more than he needed. Typical provisions for an ocean trip in the fifteenth century would include food (much of it in the form of dried meat or fruits), drink (wine and water), tools (for repairing the ships and carrying on daily routine activities), material for repairs (extra canvas for sails, planks, nails, etc.), and items for trade (beads, small bells, etc.). Water was replaced or replenished whenever the ships found land. Fresh meat and vegetables would also be brought aboard when in a port. At sea, the diet was added to by fish caught daily. Basically, Christopher was responsible for the safety and health of ninety men, and he had to have supplies necessary to support them for the entire trip.

floating by the ships, as well as bits of wood, one of which looked as if it had been carved.

That evening at vespers, special prayers of thanksgiving were said. Now the signs of land were so many that Columbus doubled the number of men on watch that night and reminded them that the first person to sight land would receive 10,000 maravedies (the unit of money used in Spain at that time) from the Spanish monarchs.

The night settled in, and everyone watched in anticipation. Then Columbus himself saw something:

*About ten o'clock at night, while standing on the sterncastle, I thought I saw a light to the west. It looked like a little wax candle bobbing up and down. It had the same appearance as a light or torch belonging to fishermen or travelers who alternately raised and lowered it, or perhaps were going from house to house. I am the first to admit that I was so eager to find land that I did not trust my own senses, so I called for Pedro Gutierrez, the representative of the King's household, and asked him to watch for the light. After a few moments, he saw it, too.*

This light was probably a bonfire on San Salvador Island. The natives frequently built fires to ward off mosquitoes and to light the evening darkness. Modern inhabitants of the island still do.

No one else, however, saw the little light. Columbus was disappointed, and everyone settled back into their watch. But in a few more hours, the great event happened. Columbus records it for us in his log:

*The moon, in its third quarter, rose in the east shortly before midnight. . . . Then, at two hours after midnight, the Pinta fired a cannon, my prearranged signal for the sighting of land. . . . When we caught up with the Pinta, which was always running ahead because she was a swift sailor, I learned that the first man to sight land was Rodrigo de Triana, a seaman from Lepe. I hauled in all sails but the mainsail to lay-to until daylight. The land is about 6 miles to the west.*

The next morning, the landfall was clearly visible. Everyone rejoiced! Columbus had proved that you could sail across the Ocean Sea. He, of course, assumed he had arrived at islands off the coast of Asia, when in reality he had discovered the islands off the land mass of the Western Hemisphere. By prearranged agreement with the king and queen, Columbus became Admiral of the Ocean Sea the day he found land across the Atlantic.

Early in the morning, Christopher and his party made for the land. He later wrote:

*At dawn we saw naked people, and I went ashore in the ship's boat, armed with swords, followed by Martín Alonso Pinzón, captain of the Pinta, and his brother, Vicente Yáñez Pinzón, captain of the Niña. I unfurled the royal banner and the captains brought the flags which displayed a large green cross with the letters F and Y* [F for Ferdinand and Y for Isabella. In the Spanish language of the fifteenth century, Isabella was spelled Ysabella] *at the left and right side of the cross.*

*... After a prayer of thanksgiving I ordered the captains of the Pinta and Niña, together with Rodrigo de Escobedo (secretary of the fleet), and Rodrigo Sanchez of Segovia (comptroller of the fleet) to bear faith and witness that I was taking possession of this island for the King and Queen. I made all the necessary declarations and these testimonies carefully written down by the secretary. ... To this island I gave the name San Salvador in honor of our Blessed Lord.*

## Where Did Columbus Land?

One of the most fascinating aspects of Columbus's voyage to scholars and laymen alike has been to try to identify on which island Christopher first landed. The log gives us general descriptions of the island, but many islands could fit his text. The only agreement among those who have studied the problem seems to be that he landed somewhere in the Bahamas group. In the Bahamas, there are thirty-six islands and 687 cays all similar in their biological, geological, and cultural makeup. Many, of course, do not fit the physical description given in the log and can be discounted. But which is the island the natives called Guanahani and Columbus named San Salvador? The issue is hotly debated by seamen, geographers, historians, anthropologists, and many peoples from all walks of life who make a hobby of trying to identify the correct island.

The island that has received the most votes is the modern island named San Salvador, which used to be called Watling Island. Other islands, however, that have been claimed, based on various reasons and evidences, are Cat Island, Grand Turk, Mayaguana, Samana Cay, Conception, Caicos, Plana Cays, and Egg Island. Professor Robert Fuson, whose translation of the log we have used, has given the most recent summary of data relating to each of these landfall theories in an appendix to his translation.

In 1985, the National Geographic Society supported new research into this problem and concluded that the right island is not an island at all, but one of the many cays. A cay is a coral reef or sand bar large enough to form a small island. Exhaustive computer studies and archaeological evidence pointed to Samana Cay, south of San Salvador Island. To date, the National Geographic landfall theory is still hotly debated and has not won too many adherents.

Following the formalities of claiming this island for his sovereigns, Christopher then met the native peoples who had witnessed these strangers on their beaches. One can only wonder what they thought about these men who had arrived in large ships, wore unusual clothes, and held a ceremony on their beach!

At first, they thought that these strange men had come from out of the sky. Christopher describes the scene for us as the indigenous people began to appear on the beach, and how they tried to communicate:

*No sooner had we concluded the formalities of taking possession of the island than people began to come to the beach, all as naked as their*

*This de Bry woodcut shows an imagined portrayal of the landing of Columbus at San Salvador Island. The natives in the picture meet him with gifts.*

*mothers bore them, and the women also, although I did not see more than one very young girl. All those that I saw were young people, none of whom was over 30 years old. They are very well-built people, with handsome bodies and very fine faces, though their appearance is marred somewhat by very broad heads and foreheads, more so than I have ever seen in any other race. Their eyes are large and very pretty, and their skin is the color of Canary Islanders or of sunburned peasants, not at all black, as would be expected because we are on an east-west line with Hierro in the Canaries. These are tall people and their legs, with no exceptions, are quite straight, and none of them has a paunch. They are, in fact, well proportioned. Their hair is not kinky, but straight, and coarse like horsehair. They wear it short over the eyebrows, but they have a long hank in the back that they never cut. Many of the natives paint their faces; others paint their whole bodies; some, only the eyes or nose. Some are painted black, some white, some red; others are of different colors. The people here called this island Guanahani in their language, and their speech is very fluent, although I do not understand any of it. They are friendly and well dispositioned people who bare no arms except for small spears, and they have no iron. I showed one my sword, and through ignorance he grabbed it by the blade and cut himself. Their spears are made of wood, to which they attach a fish tooth at one end, or some other sharp thing.*

Columbus gave the native peoples gifts and recorded in his log that they easily could be converted to Christianity because of their gentle nature. The sailors traded trinkets, such as glass beads, with the natives, in exchange for parrots, balls of cotton thread, spears, and other items. Christopher decided to take at least six of the island people back to Spain to meet the king and queen and to teach them the Christian faith and the Spanish language.

Christopher was also excited because some of the natives were wearing gold jewelry: "I have seen a few natives who wear a little piece of gold hanging from a hole made in the nose." But it was soon evident to him that there was little gold on San Salvador. It must have come from somewhere else.

# Who Were the Natives on Guanahani?

The native peoples who inhabited the islands visited by Columbus were from the Arawak language group of the Taino culture. These people had migrated north from South America into the Caribbean islands over several centuries. They were especially noted for their broad foreheads, which were a result of deliberately compressing the heads of newborn babies. Guanahani was their word for the *iguana,* a kind of lizard that lived there. Today, the iguana is an endangered species in the islands.

These people's life-style was primitive compared to the Spaniards', but Columbus did notice that the culture was more advanced on the larger islands of Cuba and Hispaniola. There they lived in villages in huts constructed from palm leaves, poles, and reeds. At the center of the village was the house of the chief, who was called the *cacique,* and in front of his house was a large open space, or plaza, where the villagers could meet. According to Columbus, they were a peaceful people given to friendliness. Other groups on the larger islands were somewhat more hostile; and, of course, the fiercest of all were the Caribes, who were cannibals. The Caribes lived on some of the islands south of what is today Cuba. They captured natives of other islands for slaves and sometimes fattened them up to eat.

In the long run, their friendliness and peacefulness were not good for these native people, as later Spanish colonists would exploit and enslave them. They were especially susceptible to the diseases, such as measles and smallpox, brought to them by the colonists.

By October 14, he was getting restless. He had fully explored the small island and knew that Asia was still at some distance. Marco Polo, whose book about Asia was one of Columbus's favorites, said that there were more than seven thousand islands in a long arch off the coast of China to the north, with Japan slightly closer and to the south. By sign language, the natives clearly indicated that there were many more islands to the south and west, some very large, and maybe even a mainland. They also indicated that that was where the gold came from.

It was time to get on with the journey. Christopher had to find

*Early woodcut illustration of natives in a canoe. Native peoples canoed between the islands of the Caribbean in vessels made from hollowed-out logs. These dugouts were used for fishing along the coast. Sometimes they were used to trade with other islands. On the fourth voyage, when Columbus was stranded on Jamaica, canoes like these were tied together in order to form a larger craft to send two sailors to Hispaniola to seek rescue.*

either the island of Japan (Cipangu) or the mainland of Asia, and he wanted to find gold to take back to his monarchs. He also carried a letter from the king and queen to the Great Khan of China that he wanted to deliver. So on October 15, the three small ships set sail once more on a southwesterly course.

By late afternoon, they sighted a larger island, which Christopher named Santa Maria de la Concepcion (the modern island of Rum Cay). Rounding the southwest point of the island, he spotted another, even larger island to the west. Investigation of Santa Maria Island proved that it was not Japan and that there was no gold there.

Christopher sailed to the larger island on October 16. This island he named Fernandia (modern-day Long Island) after his king, Ferdinand. Here Christopher made a lengthy entry into his log about the island and its people. After spending the night offshore, he began with a description of events at first light and then elaborated about the land and its inhabitants:

*As was my custom, I ordered each person to be given something, if only a few beads, 10 or 12 glass ones that cost a penny or two, and some eyelets for lacing shirts and shoes. . . . At 9 o'clock in the morning I sent the ship's boat ashore for water, and those on the island, with very good will, showed my people where the water was. They even carried the full casks to the boat and took great delight in pleasing us. . . . I must move on to discover others and to find gold. Since these people know what gold is, I know that with our Lord's help I cannot fail to find its source. Fernandia is very large and I have determined to sail around it. Although I know that Japan is to the south or southwest, and that I am about to take a detour, I understand that there is a mine of gold either in Fernandia or near it.*

As he sailed, Columbus continued to write in his log and reflect on the things he had seen thus far:

*All the people I have seen so far resemble each other. They have the same language and customs, except that these on Fernandia seem to be somewhat more domestic and tractable, and more subtle, because I notice that when they bring cotton and other things to the ship they drive a harder bargain than those of the first islands visited. And also, on Fernandia I saw cotton clothes made like short tunics. The people seem better disposed, and the women wear a small piece of cotton in front of their bodies. . . . I do not recognize any religion in the people, and I believe that they would turn Christian quickly, for they seem to understand things quite well. . . . Some of the ship's boys traded broken glass and bowls to them for spears. The others that had gone for the water told me that they had been in the houses and found them*

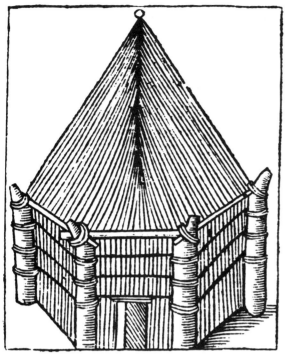

*Early woodcut drawings of native huts. Native homes took a variety of shapes. They were made of wood and palm leaves. Columbus described them as looking like Moorish tents.*

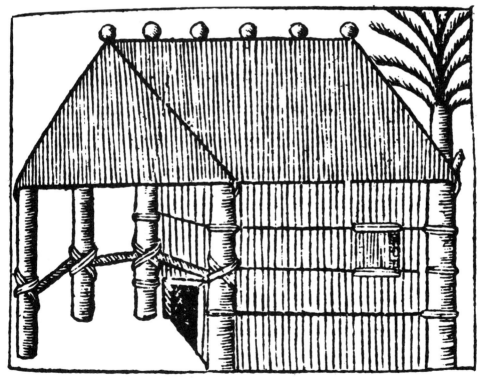

*very simple but clean, with bed and furnishings that were like nets of cotton. . . . Your Highnesses may rest assured that this land is the best and most fertile and temperate and level and good that there is in the world.*

The beds that were "like nets of cotton" were hammocks, which the natives had invented but were totally unknown in Europe. Within a short time, sailors everywhere adopted this form of bed for sleeping aboard ship. It was many times better than sleeping on the hard planks of the deck!

The natives told Christopher that gold could be found on an island they called Saomete. On October 17, he set sail for Saomete. They sailed the length of Fernandia, which took two days because the wind

*The hammock was an important contribution of native peoples to European sailors. After Columbus's voyages, ships went farther and farther, until Magellan finally circled the entire earth. Such long voyages were made much more tolerable with the hammock, since it provided comfortable sleeping on long voyages. It was easy to roll up and store during the day, and easy to put up each night.*

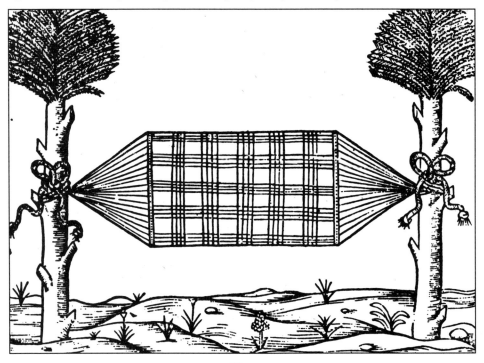

was slight, and it rained. Finally, on October 19, they left the southeast point of the island to search for Saomete. By nightfall, the island was located, and Columbus named it Isabella (modern-day Crooked Island) after the queen.

For the next couple of days, they sailed this island's coastline, and Christopher wrote many descriptions of its beauty in his log. But this island also proved not to have gold. Finally, on Sunday, Christopher believed that he had worked out a plan. He would stop sailing from island to island in a random fashion looking for gold. Instead, he would go directly south to a very large island about which the natives of all the islands had told him. They called the large island Colba (Cuba).

*I shall depart. . . . Then I shall sail for another great island which I strongly believe should be Japan, according to the signs made by the San Salvador Indians with me. They call that island Colba, where they say there are many great ships and navigators. And from that island I intend to go to another that they call Bohio, which is also very large. As to the others that lie in between, I shall see them in passing, and according to what gold or spices I find, I will determine what I must do. But I have already decided to go to the mainland and to the city of Quisay [in China] and give Your Highnesses' letter to the Grand Khan and ask for a reply and return with it.*

It was Wednesday, October 24, before he could at last sail for Colba. He proceeded on his way as fast as possible, occasionally anchoring off new islands and confirming that they did not have gold and that he was going in the right direction to reach Colba.

The more he listened to the natives, the more convinced he was that Colba was Japan. As he said on October 27, "I am now certain that Colba is the Indian name for Japan." On the next day, he found the large island. He immediately renamed it Juana after the son of Ferdinand and Isabella.

Christopher arrived at a lovely bay where a river entered the ocean. He describes it for us:

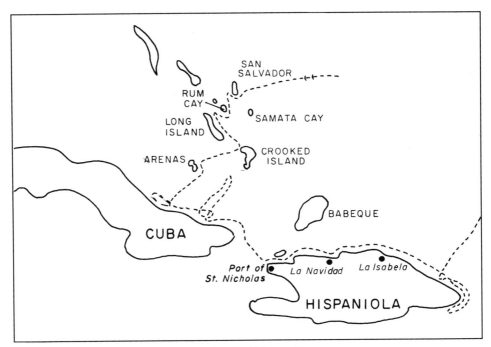

*Map of Columbus's path through the Caribbean Sea*

*I have never seen anything so beautiful. The country around the river is full of trees, beautiful and green and different from ours, each with flowers and its own kind of fruit. There are many birds of all sizes that sing very sweetly, and there are many palms different from those in Guinea or Spain. . . . I took the small boat ashore and approached two houses that I thought belonged to fishermen. The people fled in fear. In one of the houses we found a dog that did not bark.*

A dog that did not bark? Christopher records this strange animal more than once. Scholars have always been puzzled by this statement by Christopher. What kind of animal did he actually see? We probably will never know.

As beautiful as this bay was, it was not the center of a great civilization, which is what Columbus had expected to find. After a short exploration of the river, he ordered his ships to move on the next day, sailing eastward to try to find the city of the Great Khan.

He sailed all week along the coast without finding it. Finally, on

Friday, he organized a search party to go over land into the interior to try and find the Great Khan's city:

*I decided to send an embassy into the country. . . . I gave them strings of beads to trade for something to eat . . . and told them to return in six days' time. . . . I instructed them as to how they should ask for the king of that land and what they should say on the part of the Sovereigns of Castile. That is I told them to explain how the Sovereigns had sent me, in order that I might give to the king, on their behalf, their letters and a gift, and in order that I might learn of his condition and win his friendship.*

While he waited, Christopher explored the land and studied the people who lived there:

*These people are very meek and shy: naked, as I have said, without weapons and without government. These lands are very fertile. They are full of niames [sweet potatoes] which are like carrots and taste like chestnuts. They have beans very different from ours, and a great deal of cotton, which they do not sow and which grows in the mountains to the size of large trees . . . and a thousand other kinds of fruit which I cannot describe, but which should all be very profitable.*

The search party returned on November 5. All they had found was a native village of some fifty huts and no Great Khan. The only thing that they encountered that would have lasting significance was tobacco. The natives rolled the tobacco leafs into a cigar shape. They stuck them up their noses and smoked them that way!

Disappointed, Christopher sailed again on November 12. This time he went east, for the natives had declared that the next large island was where the gold could be found. "They indicated by signs that the people of that island gather gold by candlelight at night in the sand and then with a hammer make bars of it."

Christopher did not sail directly to the next large island. On the way were many islands, and his love of nature and the beauty of the

*Early woodcut of a native smoking. The first time Europeans saw natives smoking tobacco was during the first voyage. The habit was quickly adopted by explorers and early colonists and was soon introduced into Europe. The tobacco industry would become one of the largest enterprises in the New World.*

various islands delayed him for several days as he explored them. On November 19, he decided he could delay no longer. He must set out for the island the natives called Bohio (the modern-day island divided by Haiti and the Dominican Republic).

His plan was to return to the coast of Cuba, to sail to its eastern tip, and then to continue on to Bohio. But Martín Pinzón, captain of the *Pinta*, had other ideas. Without Columbus's permission, the *Pinta* left the small fleet and set out directly for Babeque to the north of Bohio, where Martín hoped to find gold. Although Martín Pinzón had been Christopher's supporter back in Palos and had convinced his fellow townsmen to follow the Genoese explorer on his adventure, the two sea captains had not gotten along well during the voyage.

Christopher sailed back to Cuba, sailed along its northern coast to its eastern tip, and stopped several times to explore inlets and bays along the way. It was not until December 5 that he finally had the proper winds to cross from Cuba to the large island known as Bohio.

The native people that Columbus had taken on board became very frightened. Columbus tells us why:

*They call it Bohio and say that it is inhabited. The people of Cuba and those of all the other islands . . . are very much afraid of the people of Bohio. They believe that those of Bohio eat people.*

But this was not so. The natives on Bohio were not the cannibals. The Caribes, who did eat people, lived on islands farther south.

The ships arrived off the coast of Bohio just before nightfall. Since

*Early woodcut of a Caribe feast of humans. Europeans thought that many of the New World groups of native peoples were cannibals. This was not true. In the area discovered by Columbus, only the fierce Caribes ate human flesh. Either they ate captured warriors from other tribes, or they kidnapped children from other groups, fattened them, and ate them at major feasts.*

it was too dark to try to make it to harbor, they stayed at sea until the next morning. On December 6, Columbus sailed until he found an excellent harbor on the western side of Bohio. He named the island Hispaniola, and the harbor he entered Port of St. Nicholas because it was the feast day of St. Nicholas.

On December 7, he left the harbor and processed along the northern coast of the island. He visited native villages when he could, and from various signs he decided gold was produced farther east. More and more gold was seen worn by the natives, and the sailors traded whatever they could for it.

On December 23, he received messengers sent from the native chief of the whole central part of the island, who had heard about the strangers sailing along their coast. Christopher became convinced that this island must be Japan and that the central part was filled with gold mines.

Unknown to him, Christopher was heading for his first serious accident. Everyone was tired. It had been a hectic two days of visits from representatives of the island's chief. The weather had been rough, making it impossible to sleep, and it was Christmas Eve. The sailors had celebrated Christmas Eve with a big party.

The winds had calmed, and the ocean became quiet. The course had been checked by sailors who had gone in the ship's small landing boat to take the island chief's representatives back to their homeland. After the eleven o'clock night watch changed, Christopher looked out at the sea and saw that it would be smooth sailing. He talked to his pilot a few minutes and then went below deck to get some much-needed rest. Other seamen soon were asleep too.

Even the helmsman was drowsy. He was falling asleep at the steering wheel. He wakened one of the ship's boys to hold the giant steering wheel while he curled up in the steerage cabin to nap. The boy could not even see over the huge railing to watch what was ahead, but that did not matter. All he had to do was keep a steady course on a calm sea.

This was the way boys learned to steer the large ships. In moments of quiet sea, late at night, when there was no danger, they were allowed to practice steering. Christopher had probably learned the same way many years before. But on this journey, Christopher had forbidden the practice of letting boys guide the ships under any circumstance. He could not risk it. They were too far from home and in unknown regions. The pilot disobeyed his orders, sure that no one would know.

Just after midnight, on December 25, Christmas Day, it happened. The *Santa María* hit a coral reef! No one knew the reef was there. Even Christopher, who had almost a sixth sense about such things, had not suspected it. It was not a hard crash; the *Santa María* slid up on the coral so slowly and silently that no one was even awakened. The boy holding the rudder knew, however, as he felt the rudder come to ground. He yelled out that the ship had hit a reef.

Christopher was the first on deck. He describes the disaster to us:

*I sailed in a light wind yesterday . . . and at the passing of the first watch, 11 o'clock at night, I was three miles east of the point. I decided to lie down to sleep because I had not slept for two days and one night.*

*This is a nineteenth-century artist's idea of how the* Santa María *might have looked as she hit a reef off the coast of Hispaniola.*

*Since it was calm, the sailor who was steering the ship also decided to catch a few winks and left the steering to a young ship's boy, a thing which I have always expressly prohibited throughout the voyage. It made no difference whether there was wind or calm; the ships were not to be steered by young boys. . . . The Lord willed that at midnight, when the crew saw me lie down to rest and also saw that there was a dead calm and the sea was as in a bowl, they all lay down to sleep and left the helm to that boy. The currents carried the ship upon one of these banks. Although it was night, the sea breaking on them made so much noise that they could be heard and seen at a three mile distance. The ship went upon the bank so quietly that it was hardly noticeable. When the boy felt the rudder ground and heard the noise of the sea, he cried out. I jumped up instantly; no one else had yet felt that we were aground.*

Christopher immediately launched men in a small boat to row around the ship to check the damage. Instead, these sailors began rowing for the *Niña* and its safety! The crew of the *Niña*, however, refused to let them on board and made them return to help their own ship. The *Santa María* was beyond saving:

*I did the only thing I could. I ordered the mast cut and the ship lightened as much as possible, to see if it could be refloated. But the water became even more shallow, and the ship settled more and more to one side. Although there was little or no sea, I could not save her. Then the seams opened, though she remained in one piece.*

Now the entire crew went aboard the *Niña* to wait for morning. As the dawn broke, Christopher sent a rowboat with his representatives to meet with the island chief, explain the disaster, and ask for help in unloading the *Santa María*. The chief sent many large canoes and came himself to help with the unloading. Everything was taken to shore, and Christopher tells us that "not even a shoe string was lost." Fortunately, there was a village nearby, and Columbus was able to store the contents of the *Santa María* in and around some of the huts.

Now there was a real problem. With the *Santa María* wrecked, there would not be room for everyone to return to Spain. Some would have to stay behind. Christopher spent the next day negotiating with the island's chief to allow some of his men to remain. The island natives he had chosen to take to Spain, however, would not be left behind. He wished to show them to the king and queen. He ordered that the crew begin to build a fortress from the beams of the *Santa María*.

# Where are the *Santa María* and La Navidad?

Many people have wanted to find the wreck of the *Santa María*. The reefs off northern Haiti have been searched in hopes of locating some remains of the famous ship. New efforts are being made by underwater archaeologists to locate her, but there may not be much to find. As Christopher tells us in the log, all her supplies were carried ashore and much of the timber of the ship was used to construct La Navidad. But the search continues for any remains.

La Navidad, the first European fort built in the New World, has not been located either. When Columbus returned a year later to this colony, he found that it had been burned down and all thirty-nine of the sailors left behind had been killed by the native people. The small settlement was built next to a large native village, and later a Spanish settlement was constructed near the site. The remains probably were farmed over many times, destroying its location. Renewed archaeological investigation began in 1983 without concrete results, but in 1986 an abandoned and silted-in well was located containing pig bones, which meant that Europeans as well as others had used the old well and thrown garbage down it. Live pigs had been part of the ships' food supply. Pigs were not native to the New World. The digging continues today with the hope that the foundations to the first fort will be found.

Thus, the first European fortress in the New World was erected on the northern coast of Hispaniola (Haiti) soon after Christmas Day in 1492. Columbus named it La Navidad (Christmas). Christopher and the island chief became good friends during the days that followed, and the natives helped the sailors build their fort.

Word now arrived that the *Pinta* was only a few miles ahead, anchored at the mouth of another river. Christopher sent letters to Martín Pinzón asking him to rejoin the *Niña*. But Pinzón ignored the request.

The fort was finished by January 2, and Christopher decided that it was time to start the long journey back to Spain. The *Pinta* still had not joined him. The sea was rough, and the wind was blowing to the east, making his departure impossible. Then on January 4, the sea calmed and the wind changed. Christopher weighed anchor and sailed east along the coast of Hispaniola.

Two days later, the *Pinta* appeared, and Martín Pinzón came aboard the *Niña* to ask forgiveness for sailing off without permission. Christopher had little choice but to forgive the other captain, as they needed each other for the trip home.

Before they left the coast of Hispaniola, however, they had to gather supplies and water for the trip; and since both the *Niña* and *Pinta* were leaking badly, they had to find a suitable beach to dock the ships and recaulk them. Finally, on January 16, everything was ready, and they sailed out into the ocean away from the new world they had discovered.

Christopher had no doubts that he would find his way home. In his log under the date of January 14, he explains his confidence:

*I have faith in Our Lord that He who brought me here will lead me back in His pity and mercy, for His Divine Majesty well knows how much controversy I had before starting from Castile, and no one else was supportive of me except God, because He knew my heart; and after God, Your Highnesses supported me, but everyone else opposed me without any reason whatsoever. . . . Almighty God will take care of everything.*

*A woodcut depicting the building of La Navidad. This scene, carved by an artist who had never been there, depicts the settlement as a European fort under construction. In reality, a wooden stockade was built around a few huts for the sailors who had been left behind.*

It was more than faith in God, however, that gave Columbus confidence that he could find a course back to Spain. One of the major reasons the monarch's advisers had recommended against the trip had been their belief that the winds blew east to west, making it impossible to sail the ships back to Spain. But Columbus knew that there were winds blowing in the opposite direction to the north. He had observed them on his trip to England and Iceland. Thus, his course was set to the northeast.

The pages of the log are sparse for the first several days of the return trip. Entries have to do with wind and sea conditions with little comment on anything else. The ships did pass through many schools of fish, including tuna, which supplemented the food stores on board. Mostly, Christopher had provisioned the ships with bread made by the island natives and sweet potatoes.

At the thirty-first parallel, Columbus turned his ships on a course due east and caught the winds he sought to sail them back to Spain.

On February 6, in fact, they made the fastest time of the entire journey, going some 275 nautical miles in a single day.

By February 7, they were sure that they had passed the westernmost island of the Azores, which they did not see but calculated was north of them. A few days later, on February 12, the sea began to get rough and the winds strong. On February 13, Christopher tells us:

*From sunset yesterday until sunrise this morning I experienced great difficulty with the wind, high waves, and a stormy sea. There has been lightning three times toward the northeast, which is a sure sign that a great storm is coming from that direction or from the direction contrary to my course. I went with bare masts most of the night, then raised a little sail and went about 39 miles. The wind abated a little today; then it increased and the sea became terrible with the waves crossing each other and pounding the ships.*

To make matters worse, the *Pinta* became separated from the *Niña* in the storm. Christopher would not know until he got back to Spain whether or not the *Pinta* had survived.

February 14 was a day of one of the worst storms Columbus or any of the other sailors had ever seen. It is best described in his own words:

*The wind increased last night, and the waves were frightful, coming in opposite directions. They crossed each other and trapped the ship, which could not go forward nor get out from between them, and the waves broke over us. . . . The wind and the sea increased greatly, and seeing the great danger I began to run before the wind, letting it carry me wherever it wanted for there was no other remedy. . . . After sunrise the wind became stronger and the crossing waves more terrible.*

Everyone was frightened and sure that the ships would sink. Columbus again called on God's help as he explained:

*I ordered that a pilgrimage to Santa Maria de Guadalupe be pledged, during which a wax candle weighing five pounds should be carried, and that each man should swear that whoever is chosen by lot will fulfill this promise. For this reason I ordered that a chick-pea be brought for every man on board; one was marked by a knife with the sign of the cross, and they were shaken up in a cap. I was the first person to draw, and it was I who took out the pea marked with the sign of the cross. Thus I was elected by chance, and from that time I considered myself obliged to fulfill the vow and make the pilgrimage.*

As the day wore on, several more lots were drawn to go on pilgrimage to various holy sites. When Christopher returned to Spain, he fulfilled his vow and visited the shrine of Guadalupe. Within a century, Our Lady of Guadalupe would become the patron saint for much of Latin America. This is her first connection with the New World.

Even though several religious vows were made, the storm did not let up. Columbus continues to describe the events of that day:

*Besides the general vows made in common, each man made his own personal vow, for none of them expected to escape, and all were resigned to being lost due to the terrible storm we were experiencing. The danger was further increased by the fact that the ship was short of ballast, since the load had been lightened by the consumption of the provisions, water and wine. . . . I also feel great anxiety because of the two sons I have in Cordoba at school, if I leave them orphaned of father and mother in a foreign land. And I am concerned because the Sovereigns do not know the service I have rendered on this voyage and the very important news I am carrying to them. . . . [So that] if I am lost in this storm the Sovereigns might have information about my voyage, I have written on a parchment everything I can concerning what I have found, earnestly beseeching whomsoever might find it to carry it to Your Highnesses. I sealed the parchment in a waxed cloth, tied it very securely, took a large wooden barrel, and placed the parchment in the barrel, without anyone knowing what it was . . . and had it thrown into the sea.*

❊   ❊   ❊

To this day, no one has ever found the barrel and its message. Finally, on February 15, the storm cleared, and the *Niña* had survived. At sunrise, an island was sighted to the northeast. Christopher was sure that the island was one of the Azores and made for it, but the sea was rough, and it took the next day and night to reach the island. At last, on Monday, February 18, they were able to anchor the ship and send a small party ashore to see where they were. Later, Columbus learned that it was the Portuguese island of Santa Maria, the easternmost island of the Azores. The people on the island said that the storm they had just come through was the worst they had ever seen.

Now a new problem arose. The king of Portugal had sent out word to all the islands he governed to detain Columbus if he was located. The interlude at the Portuguese island of Santa Maria became one of intrigue, with the Portuguese captain of the island, João de Castanheira, trying to capture Columbus and his crew.

Christopher was first aware of danger when the shore party failed to return. The captain of the island sent word that he wished them to stay ashore with him so that he could hear their stories of discovery. Columbus agreed to the request.

The next day, several sailors sought permission to go on pilgrimage to a small shrine dedicated to the Virgin Mary on the island. They wanted to give thanks for their safe passage through the storm. Columbus described what happened in his log:

*The first half of the crew went in their shirts to fulfill their vow, and while praying they were attacked and seized by all the villagers, on horseback and on foot, and by the captain as well. At the time I did not know this and remained, unsuspectingly, until 11 o'clock in the morning, expecting the boat to return so that I might go myself with the other people to fulfill our vow. When I saw that our people did not return, I suspected that they were detained or that the boat had wrecked, since the entire island is surrounded by very high cliffs. I was not able to see what was going on because the hermitage is behind a point. I raised anchor and set sail directly toward the hermitage. It was then that I saw many horsemen, well armed, who dismounted, got into the boat, and came to the ship to take me.*

The Portuguese captain and several of his men rowed out and asked Columbus to return with them. Christopher tried to lure him aboard to capture him, but the captain stayed well away from the *Niña*. Columbus continued:

*When I saw that the captain was not going to get too close, I asked him to explain why he was detaining my people. I told him that this action would surely annoy the King of Portugal, and that in the land of the Sovereigns of Castile the Portuguese are well treated, and they can come and go and are as safe as they are in Lisbon. I also told him that the Sovereigns had given us letters of recommendation for all the Princes and Lords and men in the world, which I would show him if he would approach. I informed the captain that I was Your Highnesses' Admiral of the Ocean Sea and Viceroy of the Indies. . . . I also told the captain that even if he would not surrender my people, I was not going to give up going to Castile, since I had sufficient people to navigate to Seville. And I promised him that he and his people would be severely punished for insulting us in this manner.*

The captain, however, refused to listen and told Columbus that everything he had done had been authorized by his king. Nothing was resolved, and the captain returned to the island.

A new storm came up, and Christopher had to sail back out to sea to wait out the weather. By Friday, he could return, and this time he was met by two priests and a secretary to the captain, who asked to see his royal letters. Christopher showed them the documents, and they went back to shore and released their Spanish prisoners. Christopher decided to sail out of the Azores as soon as possible, and within two days the winds changed, giving him his chance to continue on to Spain.

He no sooner got to sea than the weather began to change again, with new storms coming up. On February 27, he wrote, "I am very much concerned with these storms, now that I am so near the end of my journey." Then on March 3, a storm of cyclone proportion hit:

*A squall came upon me that split all the sails and I found myself in great danger. . . . Last night we experienced a terrible storm and thought we would be lost because the waves came from two directions and the wind appeared to raise the ship in the air, with the water from the sky and the lightning in every direction.*

When the sun came up on the next day, however, they found themselves just outside the harbor entrance to Lisbon in Portugal. On March 5, Christopher sailed into the harbor and was met by a large warship of the Portuguese. Immediately, the captain of the warship demanded that Columbus come aboard and report to the king's advisers. Columbus refused, again offering his letters from the king and queen of Spain for safe passage in foreign territory. After some consideration, the captain honored Columbus's letters and came out to his ship with great ceremony of welcome.

Word spread fast throughout Lisbon, and people began to come out to see the returned sailors and the native people they had brought from across the Ocean Sea. In fact, the king of Portugal seems to have had a change of heart about Christopher and, on March 8, sent him a letter to come to the royal court and tell him about his trip. Columbus arrived at the court on March 9:

*The King ordered that I should be received with great honor by the principal personages of his household, and he himself received me with great honor and showed me much respect. . . . He told me that he would order everything done which would be of use to Your Highnesses and to your service. . . . He indicated that he was greatly pleased that the voyage had been accomplished successfully. . . . [Sunday, March 10] Today after Mass, the King told me again that if I needed anything he would give it to me at once. And he talked with me a great deal more about the voyage . . . paying me great honor.*

On March 13, Christopher raised anchor and set sail for Palos in Spain. He arrived two days later. As if by a miracle, the *Pinta* arrived later the same day. It too, with all its sailors, had survived the storms. It was a most happy day in the small port city of Palos as fathers and sons returned after the long months at sea.

The log ends here. But other sources tell us about the triumphant return of Christopher Columbus and his sailors. There were many parties and banquets around Palos for the returning sailors. They had been gone for months, and no one knew whether they were alive or dead. They had returned with great news—they had conquered the great Ocean Sea. They had sailed across it and back.

Christopher sent a letter to the monarchs at his first opportunity informing them of his success. The royal court was at Barcelona at the other end of Spain. Columbus stayed at La Rábida monastery for several days, visiting with his friend, Friar Perez, who had helped so much in getting the king and queen's permission and support for the trip.

On Palm Sunday, he went to Seville with the natives whom he had brought back. Shortly after Easter Sunday, the monarchs answered his letter, requesting that he come to Barcelona and report in person his great achievement. They addressed their letter to "Don Christopher Columbus, Admiral of the Ocean Sea, Viceroy and Governor of the islands that he has discovered in the Indies." At last, the son of the cloth merchant of Genoa was a man of importance and titles.

Before leaving for Barcelona, Christopher also drew up a long memorandum for the king and queen on how to colonize the islands he had discovered. He wanted to take two thousand people immediately and establish villages and farms in the new lands. The king and queen in the meantime sent a letter to Pope Alexander VI, asking him to acknowledge Spain's right to all lands that Columbus had discovered.

Word of Christopher's great adventure and his discoveries spread fast. He had sent a letter from Lisbon to his friend and the monarch's adviser, Luis de Santangel, announcing his return and what he had found. This letter was shortly published in Barcelona and made avail-

*Coat of arms of Christopher Columbus. On May 20, 1493, the Spanish monarch granted Columbus the right to his own coat of arms. The above drawing is not his original crest, but the coat of arms he adopted in 1502. Notice the bottom two quarters. The left represents the islands in the Ocean Sea that he discovered, and the right shows anchors, which stand for his position as admiral.*

able to the reading public. Soon copies were published in Italian and Latin as well. All of Europe was being informed of the great feat of the Genoese explorer.

Christopher left for his meeting with the Spanish king and queen. He dressed now as an admiral. He traveled with many people, including the native people whom he had brought to Spain. They left Seville and made their way across the Spanish countryside, where it seemed almost every town had a parade and came to welcome him.

The greatest celebration waited for him in Barcelona, where the monarchs had the city decorated with banners. All the court came out to escort him into the city. The next day, he was received by the king and queen with great pomp and ceremony. He entered the court filled with the most important people in Spain and he, for now, was the most important of all. Everyone wanted to meet him and talk to him. How unlike the days only two years before when everyone laughed at his ideas!

He was seated next to the king and queen, an honor unheard of for a commoner. They spent hours talking about the great adventure. The monarchs examined the things he had brought back, and they met the island natives. They discussed plans to send a new expedition immediately. This time it would be a large fleet, fully paid for from the royal treasury. Columbus could have anything he wanted!

Afterward, they all went to the royal chapel to pray and give thanksgiving for the voyage. He was given living quarters in the royal household, and when the king went riding in the countryside, he wanted Columbus by his side. Never again would Christopher be treated so royally or so well. The greatest of adventures was over, but there were to be more adventures ahead.

*A nineteenth-century painting by Eugène Delacroix depicting the historical event of Columbus's return from his first voyage. The artist shows Columbus presenting the king and queen with riches and souvenirs from the New World while in the background stand the native peoples whom he brought back to show the monarchs.*

# CHAPTER FOUR

# More Adventures in the New World

Christopher had realized only part of his dream. He had sailed across the great Ocean Sea, but he had not found Asia. Still convinced that the islands he had discovered were part of a huge chain of islands off the Asian mainland, he was encouraged by the king and queen to go back as soon as possible.

This time he had full financial support from the king and queen. They agreed with his suggestion that Spain send colonists to settle in the islands he had discovered. A great expedition was to be sent from the port city of Cadiz. In June 1493, Columbus left the court to prepare for the second voyage to the New World.

The king and queen wanted him to sail immediately. They began to worry that Portugal would sail west and claim the lands Columbus had discovered. At the same time, they were negotiating an international treaty through the Catholic pope, Alexander VI, to establish a division line between Spain and Portugal in which each would have rights to discovered lands in the Ocean Sea. The end result was called the Line of Demarcation, which gave Spain rights to all lands discovered west and south of the islands found by Columbus and Portugal all territories discovered east of those lands.

For the second voyage, Columbus collected seventeen ships and about fourteen hundred people. Again, we know almost nothing about the ships, only that they seemed to be of various types. The flagship he again named the *Santa María*, and the *Niña*, which had gone on the first voyage, was included once more on this trip. Many of the sailors from the first voyage signed on to return to the New World. Also on this voyage, many sailors from Genoa, Columbus's hometown, enlisted, including Columbus's youngest brother, Giacomo. Giacomo was now known by his Spanish name, Diego.

The passengers were men of many skills. Soldiers and horses were taken, plus craftsmen, farmers, laborers, and five priests. Nearly two hundred young men of noble birth paid their own way to go for the adventure and in hopes of finding gold. The ship's doctor of the fleet was Diego Alvares Chanca, who wrote an account of this trip. Although Columbus kept a log once more, that document has also been lost. Most of what we know about this trip comes from the journal of Dr. Chanca and from a journal kept by Columbus's boyhood friend, Michele de Cuneo, who also went.

Even though the king and queen wanted the fleet to sail at once, the preparations went slowly. One reason why it took Christopher so long to get this fleet underway was that no one had ever launched a colonizing enterprise before. Supplies had to be taken to last up to two years. And besides all the people, many animals were taken to breed in the colonies—chickens, cattle, donkeys, sheep, goats, and pigs. The colonists also took supplies of seeds to plant. It was a major operation with thousands of items to be thought of and taken along to establish colonies in the islands.

The great day for sailing came on Wednesday, September 25, 1493. Christopher's two sons, Diego and Ferdinand, were at the dock and waved good-bye to their father after he had taken communion and made his confession. The fleet again sailed west to the Canary Islands to take on fresh provisions.

They arrived at Grand Canary on October 2. After five days, they sailed for the Indies on October 7. The crossing from the Canary Islands took only twenty-two days. The first island was sighted on a Sunday, so the admiral named it Dominica after the Spanish name for the day. Christopher had sailed much farther south than on the first voyage and now changed his course to the north and west, encountering many new islands. He visited many as he made his way back to Hispaniola and the men he had left at La Navidad.

By late November, the fleet was off the coast of Hispaniola, where the dead bodies of two bearded men were discovered on the beach. The native people did not wear beards, so the colonists knew that these had to be men from La Navidad. They grew apprehensive as they continued on. On the evening of November 26, they arrived outside the reefs surrounding the bay where La Navidad had been built. Cannons were fired to alert the fort, but no shot was returned. All was silent. That night a canoe of natives arrived to speak to the admiral. They said that all his men at La Navidad had died from disease and from raids by hostile natives.

*Map of the second, third, and fourth voyages*

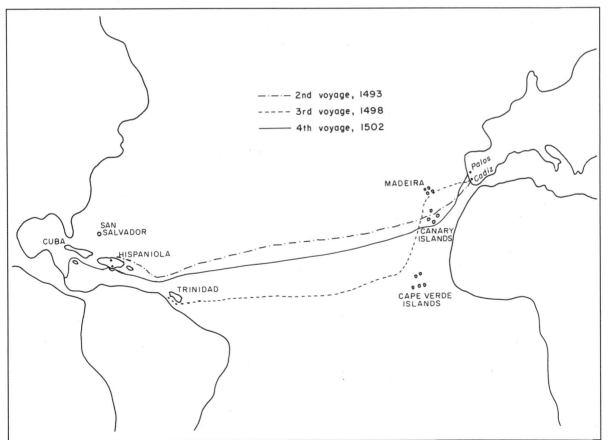

The next day, Christopher went ashore to see for himself. All he found was the burned remains of the fortress and no sign of the men he had left behind. Eleven corpses were finally located not far away and were given Christian burial.

The reports Columbus got from the natives of the island were contradictory and confusing. Some said that the Spaniards had fought among themselves; others blamed the disaster on raiding parties from other islands. Columbus suspected that the nearby villagers probably had killed them. We will never know exactly what happened. Piecing together the stories of the natives, it seems that these Spaniards had stolen women and gold from the surrounding villages.

After a few more days, Christopher decided to leave the area and search for a site to build a new colony for the many people who had come with him. The site where La Navidad had stood was no longer suitable because Christopher could no longer trust the natives. Also, he believed that there were rich gold deposits farther east on the island. They set sail again on December 7 to look for a better location.

The trip eastward was extremely difficult because of strong winds. Many people were sick, including Christopher. Finally, just before Christmas, they found a new harbor and a site that appeared suitable for building a settlement. Work was begun at once to erect fortifications and housing for men and animals. Christopher named the new colony La Isabela after the queen.

Sickness continued to plague the new settlers, including Christopher, who was ill for several weeks. In January, he sent a search party inland to look for the gold that was supposed to be there. The search party found some, but not as much as he had hoped. On February 2, he sent most of the ships back to Spain, keeping only five for further exploration. He sent with them a long letter, which is still available, requesting more supplies and suggesting better ways to colonize.

After the ships left, Columbus had some problems with his settlers and had to arrest some to stop them from rebellion. He was not a very good governor. He was not even interested in governing. He wanted to look for gold and for Asia. But he had been made viceroy, or governor, over all the lands he found, and he tried to keep peace and

# What Did the Ships Carry Back to Spain?

The accomplishment of Christopher Columbus was more than just sailing across the Ocean Sea and discovering new lands. He made it possible for others to do so too. From this time on, Spanish ships made the voyage to the Caribbean islands on a regular basis and, within time, to the mainland of South and Central America as well. What did ships bring to the New World, and what did they take back? Obviously, Spain wanted as much gold as possible and, later on, as much silver as the ships could carry.

In the early years, ships brought supplies for the colonists and items that could be traded to the natives. One of the earliest records of transatlantic shipping is a letter sent by Christopher Columbus to the king and queen requesting supplies during his second voyage. Most of what he wanted were items necessary for the new colony of La Isabela: wine, salted meat, salt, guns and powder, sheep, goats, pigs, donkeys, and cattle. He sent the letter back to Spain with twelve ships loaded with goods.

The ships docked at Cadiz on February 2, and the king and queen sent a royal secretary to record the items on board. This document survives too. This was the first load of goods from the new lands. (The things brought back on the first voyage were mostly to show what Columbus had found.) The royal secretary recorded that the ships unloaded about 240 pounds of gold, cartons of cinnamon, ginger, pepper, piles of sandalwood, bales of cotton and woven cloth, sixty parrots, and twenty-six native people (three of them considered to be cannibals).

order. His lack of success, however, would be the worst mark on his record and cause him many problems in the years ahead.

A few days later, he took five hundred of his men and marched inland, looking for the wealth of the gold mines he was sure would be there. In the middle of the island, he established another fort and village, which he named St. Thomas. He left about fifty men there to search for gold. He returned to La Isabela to find the settlers again near rebellion. He settled the problems with them and was now ready to explore the islands farther. He left his brother Diego in command of the colony and sailed on April 14 to try to find the Asian mainland.

# The Colony of La Isabela

La Navidad, the fort built to house sailors left behind on the first voyage, was not a planned colony; rather, it was meant as a temporary refuge. After he discovered La Navidad burned to the ground and the sailors all dead, Columbus sailed farther along the coast to the east to look for a site for the first real colony in the New World. He chose what he considered one of the most beautiful harbors he had ever seen, on the north coast of Hispaniola about halfway across the island. Here he and the others set to work building a permanent settlement to house nearly fourteen hundred people, and named it La Isabela for their queen.

Almost immediately, however, the colonists, including Christopher, fell very ill. No one knows for sure what made them sick, but it has been suggested that the food they were buying from the natives—cassava bread, maize (corn), sweet potatoes—was tainted or disagreed with their body systems. Cassava bread was frequently eaten by the Spaniards. It is made from the poisonous roots of the yucca or manioc, but the poison is leached out before it is kneaded into dough, patted into thin pancake, and cooked on a griddle.

The unusually high fever along with diarrhea also suggests dysentery. Malaria is another good possibility, for the new settlers were plagued by swarms of mosquitoes almost from the beginning. Whatever it was, several hundred fell ill, and many died.

Columbus sailed to the western end of Hispaniola and on toward Juana (Cuba), then turned south again and sailed on toward a new island named Jamaica. From there, he and his ships sailed north and again found Cuba and sailed along its southern coast. By June 12, Christopher had had enough. He had not found any riches, and the people he encountered were still primitive and poor. He was hopeful, however, that Cuba might be a part of a continent. He and his ships sailed back to Jamaica and then on to Hispaniola, along its southern coast and on around the island to the colony of La Isabela, where they

Christopher had a hard time building the small colony. Most of the settlers were too sick to work, and the soldiers and nobles refused to do manual labor. He finally had to force them to work on constructing the buildings, and before long, many of the settlers hated him. Within time, however, La Isabela grew into a small town with several hundred thatched houses, a storehouse, a small church, and an armory. Nevertheless, within a few years, the first settlement in the New World was abandoned. The site of La Isabela was beautiful, but it was too hard to grow food there. Furthermore, gold was found in the middle of the island and on the southern coast. Christopher asked his brother Bartholomew, who was to command the island in Christopher's absence, to find a new location with a good harbor along the south coast. Bartholomew found such a site on the Ozmana River. He moved the colonists there and named the new settlement Santo Domingo. Today, Santo Domingo is considered the oldest, most continuously lived-in city in the Western Hemisphere founded by Europeans.

What happened to La Isabela? Unfortunately, it was left to fall into ruins for five hundred years. Many of the buildings, such as the storehouse and hospital, had been build from rock, so the site remained in ruins until the twentieth century. In 1945, the Dominican dictator ordered all the ruins bulldozed into the sea so that the area would be clean for a visiting dignitary, thus destroying a primary archaeological site. It was not until the 1980s that serious archaeological work began on the site, with a mapping of the ruins. One of the important events of the 1992 Columbus quincentenary is to fully excavate La Isabela.

arrived on September 29. Christopher had been ill again. For several days before landing at La Isabela, he had a high fever and was delirious. He could not see, and his other senses failed him as well.

While Columbus had been exploring the islands, the supplies he had asked for had arrived. The king and queen had selected Christopher's brother Bartholomew to lead three ships to La Isabela. So when the sick Christopher returned to La Isabela, two of his brothers were there to nurse him back to health. It took several months for him to recover. In the meantime, the Spanish colonists continued to disobey

# Local Foods

Some native foods produced in the islands were delicious, and the colonists enjoyed them: potatoes, maize, melons, cucumbers, and all kinds of fruits. They especially liked pineapples, which they had never eaten before. Cassava bread was soon adopted as a staple by the colonists. Corn bread was also available. Then there were fish of all kinds to be caught in both the ocean and in freshwater rivers, as well as various birds and other animals to be hunted for food.

Several of the New World foods were introduced into countries throughout the world, adding to the basic foods we eat. Potatoes are one example. Christopher and his companions mostly saw sweet potatoes, but there were numerous varieties to choose from. Potatoes were first imported into Europe as a luxury food for the very rich, but people soon found that they grew very well in Europe, especially in northern Europe. A tiny garden of potatoes, it was soon learned, offered a higher nutritional yield per acre than anything else, including cereal grains. Potatoes survived both climate in northern Europe and the ravages of war (armies could ride over a potato field, and there would still be a crop). Within two hundred years after Columbus discovered the New World, the potato had become the chief food for peasants and poorer classes of people all over Europe. In modern times, many thousands of people have survived famine conditions because potatoes grow, almost no matter what happens.

Of all the results of Columbus's discovery, the changes made in agriculture were perhaps the most important and far-reaching. From his discovery, the vegetable resources of the European world had been doubled!

Many of the native foods, however, were repulsive to the Spanish; yet at times, they had to eat them. For example, iguana, considered a delicacy among the natives, paca, a big rodent or rat, and those "barkless dogs" never appealed to the Spanish no matter how hungry they were!

orders, and there were daily troubles for the Columbus brothers to handle.

Christopher did not wish to return to Spain after his health improved, but he had to. He did not have much gold to show the king

*Cassava bread became a staple food item for Columbus and his crews from the very beginning. It is made from the root of a plant and must have its poison removed before it is formed into dough. Natives patted the dough into a pancake shape and cooked it on a hot flat stone over a fire.*

*Early drawing of an island iguana. Iguana was a favorite food eaten by native peoples on the islands discovered by Columbus. At times the sailors, and the colonists who followed, also ate the large lizard.*

and queen, his colony was not firmly under his control, and he had not found Asia. Finally, by October 1495, he felt that things were going smoothly enough to return. He had collected some gold from the natives as tribute (taxes), and he prepared to leave. But again he delayed the trip until the spring. Finally, he left the New World and arrived back in Cadiz on June 11, 1496.

This return was not as pleasant as the one after the first voyage. There were no great parades, no parties, no ceremonies. Instead, many of those who had sailed with him on the second voyage had returned already and reported their dislike of Christopher and his way of governing the colony. Passengers on supply ships going back and forth to La Isabela had reported that political and economic conditions in the Indies were not good. Christopher fully expected the king and queen to be angry.

But this was not the case. The king and queen were astute rulers who never believed all that they heard and accepted the fact that rumors about conditions at the new colony were just rumors. They knew Columbus was a mariner and explorer, not a government bureaucrat, and they had expected some problems. The court now was at Burgos, and they sent Columbus a friendly letter asking him to attend. They assured him that he would be well received. Also, Christopher's two sons, Diego and Ferdinand, were at court assigned to serve the young Prince Juan.

Christopher was well received with all the honors due to the Admiral of the Ocean Sea. The king and queen were anxious to hear about his second voyage, and he gave them a good account. He told them that he had discovered many more islands and possibly a continent. He told them of sailing entirely around Hispaniola, which he felt was larger than all of Spain, with many natives willing to pay the king and queen taxes. He explained the problems at La Isabela as a situation where greed was stronger than the Christian faith and where many of the colonists refused to work. He ended by asking the monarchs for eight new ships for a return trip. Two would be sent immediately to La Isabela with fresh supplies, while he would take the other six and finally discover the continent.

This time he would sail much farther south, as all of his studies and conversations with natives indicated that a continent was there. The monarchs agreed and said that he would get the ships and supplies he requested. Things did not work out as everyone wanted, however. In order to protect their interests in Europe, royal marriages between Ferdinand and Isabella's children and several royal families in Portugal, England, and the Holy Roman Empire had to be made. Much money was required for these marriages, and a fleet of 130 ships was needed to take Princess Doña Juana to Flanders. Christopher had to wait until this fleet returned to get his eight ships.

Finally, on January 23, 1498, the two ships left for Hispaniola with supplies. The *Niña* was one of those ships. Christopher did not get away until four more months passed. He finally sailed down the river from Seville and reached the open sea on May 30, 1498. In the end, he was given the six ships he had requested for this trip.

The third voyage was in many ways the most important for Columbus. Its purpose was to locate a mainland, and on it he finally found the continent. It was not Asia, however. It was South America. He had sailed much farther south than before, and because the ships were now closer to the equator, it became very hot. Columbus's log of this voyage is lost also, but Bishop las Casas, who wrote from it before it disappeared, describes one unbearable period of extremely hot weather:

*So suddenly . . . did the . . . heat strike them that no one would go below decks to see to the casks of wine and water, which burst and snapped their hoops. The wheat burnt like fire; the salt pork and other meat scorched and went bad. The heat lasted for eight days.*

One theory Columbus had held, based upon the ancient writers he had read, was that there had to be a fourth continent to balance the earth. If Europe had a continent to the south, Africa, then Asia had to have a continent to its south. The theoretical continent had been named Paria. Christopher hoped to find Paria.

Christopher was ill for much of the voyage. He had arthritis, which was becoming worse. And he had continuing medical complications from a severe plague of dysentery during the second voyage.

The fleet of six ships was divided near the Canary Islands. Three headed directly for Hispaniola while three others, under the command

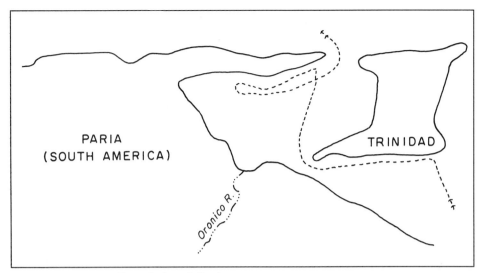

*Map of voyage to Trinidad and Paria*

of Columbus, headed farther south to explore near the equator. By the
end of July, the three ships on the discovery route were running out
of water and supplies. It was still very hot, so Columbus shifted his
course to the north and west in hopes of returning to Hispaniola or
one of the Caribe islands.

Then on July 31, one of his sailors spotted land to the north.
Christopher, who had dedicated this trip to the Holy Trinity, was awed
to see three mountains rising miraculously from the sea as if they
represented the members of the Trinity. Believing that God had led
him to this site, he named the island Trinidad in honor of the Holy
Trinity.

They sailed along the southern coast of this new island, which was
very large and very beautiful, and to the south, they could see more
land, some twenty miles away, which they thought must be another
island. When they reached the western tip of Trinidad, they entered
yellowish water that churned and swirled. The water was not very
salty, almost drinkable. Christopher sailed along the coast of the land
to the north, anchored, and sent parties of men ashore to contact the
natives.

They noticed that the people living here wore a lot of gold and pearls. The natives told him that more people lived to the west. Putting it all together, Christopher knew that the less salty water rushing into the sea, causing it to discolor, had to be a major river, which could only be from a continent. "I have come to believe that this is a vast continent, hitherto unknown. I am greatly supported in this view by the great river and by the fresh water of the sea."

Columbus had found Paria (modern-day South America). He was ecstatic and wrote to the king and queen:

*Your Highnesses have gained these immense territories which amount to another world in which Christendom will take great joy, and our Holy Faith will in time be mighty. I say this in all honor and because I wish Your Highnesses to be the greatest rulers in the world, I mean rulers of it all.*

This is the first time that Columbus hints that he had found something besides Asia. He had located "another world." He still believed that he was close to Asia, but he knew that what he had found was a continent not on the charts or in the books he had read.

He had no time to explore. He too had supplies for the settlers at Hispaniola, and those supplies were rotting. He had to get on with his trip. But as he sailed on to Hispaniola, he became ill again. This time his eyes were bleeding, and he could not see. He had time to reflect on many events of the past few days and came to an odd conclusion, which he wrote to the king and queen. He decided that he had sailed within a few miles of the biblical Garden of Eden!

He had long wanted to find this important Christian historical site. The books he had studied and the biblical passages he had read had convinced him that the location of the home of Adam and Eve still existed somewhere in the world. On the medieval maps he had studied, geographers had placed the mythical garden to the eastern fringes of Asia. Other books he had read theorized that the garden was located on top of a high mountain, so high that the garden had not been washed away in the great flood of the Old Testament. So Columbus figured that the location would be at an unusually high elevation.

As he sailed away from Trinidad, again he found the North Star was not where he expected it to be according to his compass. Reflecting on what this might mean, he arrived at a startling conclusion about the shape of the earth.

*I have always read that the world, both land and water, is spherical, as the studies of Ptolemy and the writings of all other authorities on this subject have demonstrated and proved. . . . But now . . . I have seen inconsistency* [the position of the Pole Star]. *I . . . conclude this about the earth. I have found that its shape is not that of a true sphere . . . but more like a pear . . . round except toward the stalk where it protrudes considerably, or . . . round with a protrusion on one side, like a woman's breast.*

Then Christopher wrote a long summary of what famous men had said about the location of the biblical Garden of Eden; that is, that it was located atop a rugged mountain in the east. To this, he now disagrees also. Instead, he tells the king and queen:

*I do not think that the Earthly Paradise is shaped like a rugged mountain, as the descriptions have told us, but that it is at the summit, where I have said that the point of the pear is situated . . . this river* [the Orinoco] *if it does not come from the Earthly Paradise, then it must come from an immense land in the south, about which we as yet know nothing. But I am quite convinced in my own mind that the Earthly Paradise is where I have said. . . .*

He never gave up this belief. A few years later, in 1502, he wrote a letter to Pope Alexander VI in which he told the pope that he still believed that he had located the site of the biblical Garden of Eden.

Even though sick, Columbus now made directly for Hispaniola and the new colony of Santo Domingo, where he had left his brothers in charge. Santo Domingo replaced La Isabela as the main New World colony, and it is still the major city of the modern-day country of the

*This map/drawing of the colony of Santo Domingo was done in 1619. Santo Domingo is the oldest European-founded city in the Western Hemisphere. Many of these buildings still stand today.*

Dominican Republic. After arriving there, Christopher became worried about the continued reports of rebellion among the settlers. Before he had left Spain on this voyage, returning settlers had begun to advise the king and queen that the colony was governed poorly. What he did not know was that the king and queen had finally grown alarmed by those reports and had sent their own agent, Francisco de Bobadilla, to investigate, with full powers to solve the problems he found.

The news at Santo Domingo was not good. Many settlers had died from sickness, and over a hundred more were severely ill. The Spanish settlers still disliked taking orders from the Italian Columbus brothers, whom they viewed as foreigners. Eventually, many sided against them under the leadership of Francisco Roldán, who had been named mayor of the settlement.

Roldán and his followers had first tried to leave the colony and take a boat back to Spain. Christopher's brother Bartholomew refused to permit this, and Roldán's group went inland and had made friends with native leaders who had agreed to help them in a rebellion against the Columbus brothers. After days of fighting, Bartholomew and Diego had put down the rebellion, and Roldán and his followers had fled into the mountains.

Christopher took control of the situation but handled it badly. Rather than capturing Roldán and bringing him to justice, Christopher negotiated with him, making unnecessary concessions to the rebels. Peace was restored momentarily, but within a short while the rebels again caused problems among the settlers. To make matters worse, the native groups attacked the Spanish at every opportunity. The basic problem was that the Spanish settlers wanted to be able to use the natives in any way they wished. They especially wished to make them slaves. Many of the Spanish settlers from the upper classes did not believe that they should have to work, even to help build the colony. Columbus refused to allow the Spanish settlers to take advantage of the natives, and he insisted that everyone, no matter what their social position might be, had to work. The settlers still exploited the natives at every opportunity, causing the hostility of the natives to the settlers. Christopher and his brothers tried to strengthen their rule by hanging seven of the rebels. At this point, Francisco de Bobadilla arrived to begin his investigation.

Bobadilla held a hurried investigation, believed the dissatisfied rebels, and had Christopher and his brothers arrested and put in irons. Because Christopher was a favorite at court, Bobadilla decided to send him and his brothers back to Spain to stand trial for mismanagement. Thus, Columbus was shipped back from the islands he had

*Theodore de Bry tried to capture the moment when Columbus and his brother were arrested by Bobadilla, who would send them home in chains.*

discovered in chains and humiliated. He wrote a long letter to his friend Doña Juana de Torres about these events and said,

*In Spain, they judge me as if I had been a governor in Sicily, or in some well-ordered city or town, where laws can be kept to the letter, without risking total disaster. I feel that this is completely unjust. I should be judged as a captain who has gone from Spain to the Indies, to conquer a numerous and warlike nation, whose customs and beliefs are entirely different from ours, who live in the highlands and among the mountains, with no abiding habitations, where, by the grace of God, I have brought a new world into the dominions of Our Sovereigns, the king and queen of Spain, whereby Spain, which was once held to be poor, is now the wealthiest of countries.*

Thus, he arrived back in Spain in irons late October 1500.

His third voyage, on which he had discovered a continent, ended in disaster. He was met not by parades and parties, but by royal officials to be handed over for trial.

But Bobadilla had gone too far. The king and queen were shocked that their Admiral of the Ocean Sea had been treated this way. When they got the news, they ordered the Columbus brothers to be released immediately, sent them money to buy proper clothing, and asked them to come to the court.

When Christopher and his brothers arrived at the court, they were met with great courtesy. Columbus was still well liked by the monarchs. He had done a great deal for them, and he was their Admiral of the Ocean Sea. All charges against the brothers were dropped, and all of Christopher's rights and privileges were restored, except one. He was no longer to govern the lands he had found. He still held the title of viceroy, but the monarch appointed a governor actually to rule the islands.

Columbus wanted to make another trip of discovery. It was his idea this time to sail farther west of Hispaniola and look for a passage on to Asia. He hoped he could find the passage and sail around the world.

While he waited permission for the fourth voyage, Christopher was very busy. He stayed at a monastery outside of Seville with his friend and fellow Italian Father Gaspar Gorricio. While there, he collected all the letters, memoranda, deeds, titles, and other documents that spelled out his rights and privileges and had them compiled into a book that today is called the *Book of Privileges*. Copies were made of these documents and sent to various people for safekeeping. They not only guaranteed Christopher's rights, they guaranteed those rights for his descendants.

Also, while staying in the monastery, he compiled a *Book of Prophecies* in which he outlined his desire for Christianity to be taken to all the people of the earth, especially the natives of the lands he had found; and in this book, he called for the Spanish monarchs to lead a crusade to the Holy Lands to capture them from the Moslems.

# The Juan de la Cosa Map

The map below is important for two reasons: It is the oldest surviving map showing the areas explored by Columbus, and it portrays Columbus in a religious role. Juan de la Cosa, who drew this map, was an important explorer in his own right. He was an early friend of Columbus and went with Christopher on the first voyage. In fact, he was the owner of the *Santa María,* which sank off Hispaniola in 1492. He also took part in the second voyage with Columbus. Juan returned at least two more times to the New World, once in 1499 when he sailed with Amerigo Vespucci. After four trips, Juan drew this map of the region. Symbolically, he drew on the left side of the map a picture of St. Christopher carrying the Christ child (an ancient Christian legend). This represented Christopher Columbus as the one who brought the Christian faith to the New World. Juan died in 1509 in what is now Panama, during a skirmish with native peoples.

*Map drawn by Juan de la Cosa in 1500. Today, this map is very faded and it is difficult to reproduce. It hangs in the Maritime Museum in Madrid, Spain. Notice, on the left of the map, the western islands and mainlands known to Juan de la Cosa when he drew the map. Also on the left, Juan de la Cosa pictures Christopher Columbus as Saint Christopher carrying the Christ child. This is the earliest-known map showing the New World.*

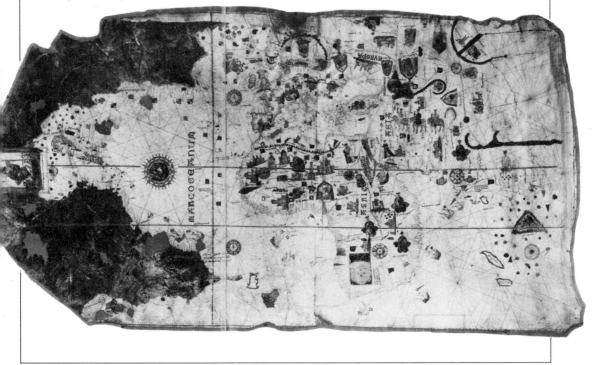

He believed that the wealth from the New World should be used for this purpose.

Christopher used the *Book of Prophecies* to express his strong belief that he had been specially chosen by God to unlock the mysteries of the Ocean Sea. He felt that his discoveries had been predicted in the Holy Bible as an event that would happen near the time of the expected Second Coming of Jesus.

Studying the chronology of final events in world history, as he interpreted them in the Bible and other writings, he told the king and queen that the world as they knew it would only last another one hundred fifty years. According to his studies and his beliefs, the Christian Gospel had to be preached to all the people of the world (the rest of whom he had found in the New World), and the holy city of Jerusalem had to be captured by Christians in order to complete preparations for Christ's Second Coming.

Columbus also changed the way he signed his name about this time. He created a strange signature that is still puzzled over. Even today, no one knows the meaning of it. It looked like this:

Many people have tried to figure out what the letters mean, but no one knows for sure. X͞po FERENS is a Greek-Latin form for Christopher meaning "Christ Bearer," but the other symbols are a mystery. Sometimes he would not end with X͞po FERENS but with Admiral or Viceroy.

Christopher's discoveries were beginning to cause a flood of exploration across the Ocean Sea. While staying at Seville, he received word that Pedro Cabral, a Portuguese explorer, had found land in the southwest (modern-day Brazil) and that Gaspar Corte-Real, another

Portuguese, had found a continent to the northwest. He was excited also by the news that another Genoese explorer, John Cabot, in the service of the king of England, had sailed across the Ocean Sea far to the north and discovered a huge continent (now the United States and Canada). The Admiral of the Ocean Sea was anxious to go again.

The king and queen approved the fourth voyage, and four ships were hired with crews and supplies. After weeks of preparation, they sailed from Cadiz on May 11, 1502. Christopher took his younger son, Ferdinand, on this trip. Information about the adventures on the fourth voyage is plentiful. We not only have a long letter from Columbus that describes the trip in some detail, but we also have the firsthand account by Ferdinand in his biography of his father. Ninety-two seamen were hired for the four ships, nearly half of whom were described as "boys." It was a young crew and not as experienced as those in the past.

Christopher named this trip the "high voyage." On it, he hoped to find a passage through the islands and land masses to Asia. He was full of hope, but he was also very ill. He could not go below deck because of his arthritis; instead, he had a special sling made to sit in above deck and a cabin on deck, "like a little doghouse," to sleep in. Once he got to the New World, he frequently had to be carried ashore because he could not walk. His eyes bled, and he had urinary problems and swollen joints. It would be his last voyage.

Christopher sailed first to Morocco in North Africa, however. He did this because a new war had broken out between Christians and Moslems, and he wanted to see the fighting for himself. Then he hurried on to the Grand Canary Island to take on fresh supplies. He sailed rapidly to the Indies, arriving at an island south of Hispaniola in just twenty-one days. He then turned north and anchored off Santo Domingo on June 29. He had been forbidden to go to Hispaniola. Even though the king and queen had erased all charges against Columbus after he returned from the third voyage, they had turned the colony over to others to administer. These administrators allowed the settlers to exploit the natives and to enslave them. Knowing that if they allowed Christopher to return to the colony the old conflicts would arise again, they had forbidden him to go there. But he had reason to disobey. One of his ships was in such bad shape that he hoped to hire another to replace it. Also, his senses told him that a major storm, a hurricane, was brewing, and he needed shelter.

The new governor of the colony sent word that there were no ships available and that he could not enter the harbor. Nor did he nor anyone else believe that a storm was approaching. In fact, the colony had a fleet of twenty-eight ships ready to sail back to Spain loaded with gold and native slaves. Because they did not believe Columbus, the fleet sailed on schedule. Aboard one of the ships was Francisco Bobadilla, the man who had sent Christopher home in chains.

Unable to enter the safety of the harbor, Christopher took his four ships farther west, down the coast, to the mouth of a river that emptied into the ocean. He sailed into the mouth of the river to wait out the storm he knew would hit. It did! Even anchored in the river mouth, Christopher barely rode out the storm. His ships were battered and broke loose from their anchors, but they all survived. The fleet that had left Santo Domingo did not fare so well. Only four of the twenty-eight ships survived. Both Bobadilla and Roldán (the rebel), who were returning to Spain, were killed, along with about five hundred others. It is estimated that two thousand pounds of gold sank with the ships! Ironically, we are told, and it may simply be a legend, one of the four ships that did survive was the one that was carrying Christopher's own gold back to Spain.

After resting a few days and repairing their ships, Christopher and his men sailed on to the southwest. They passed Jamaica and went on until they saw a long coastline with blue mountains. They had arrived at what today is Central America. Columbus was convinced that he was off the coast of Asia.

At first, he sailed north along the coast to assure himself that this was really a continent. Ironically, if he had gone north a little farther, he would have found the Mayan and Aztec civilizations of Mexico, both highly advanced, and both of which mined large quantities of gold. Instead, he turned south too soon to contact these civilizations.

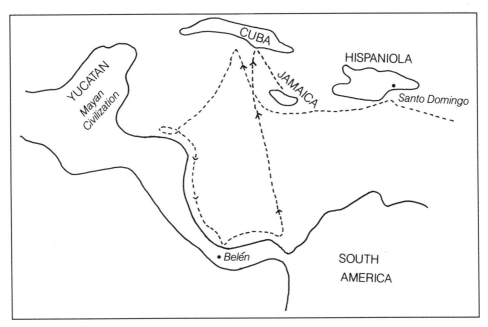

*Map of the fourth voyage*

He hoped by sailing south to find a passage to the Indian Ocean, and to return to Spain by going around the world. He sailed the coast, thinking that it would turn south and he would sail around the land mass and be on his way to the Indian Ocean. Actually, he was only a few miles from the Pacific Ocean, which was just across those mountains in Central America. The natives with whom he spoke told him that there was another great ocean just on the other side, so he knew that he was on the right track. By now, though, all of his ships were in sad shape, worm-eaten and leaking badly.

The farther south they traveled, the more gold they saw. And the natives told them that the gold came from the land of Veragua and Ciguare just ahead and over the mountain range. The natives told him also that Veragua and Ciguare were across a peninsula from each other and that they were nine days' journey from each other and on different oceans.

Columbus, of course, assumed that Ciguare was on the coast of the Indian Ocean. Further, he assumed, Ciguare must be the fabled

Chiamba of the Orient that Marco Polo had told about. Christopher was excited. The "high voyage" was finally going to accomplish his goal of reaching the rich lands of Asia.

The problem was that the Spaniards did not speak the natives' language. The natives would nod and smile at their questions, which led the Spanish to believe that the areas of Veragua and Ciguare were parts of a highly advanced civilization with trade fairs, beautiful cities, and oceangoing ships, where people wore rich clothing and were highly cultured. Christopher was optimistic, but when the coast turned southeast instead of southwest, he became worried.

Nevertheless, there seemed to be more villages both on the coast and inland up the rivers. The population was increasing, and so was the gold being worn. On February 6, Christopher anchored his ships and sent a party of men inland to talk to the natives about their gold mines. Here is his report:

*I sent seventy men into the interior, and five leagues from the shore they found many mines. The Indians who were with them led them up a very high hill. They showed them the country all around, as far as the eye could see, and said that there was gold everywhere, and that the mines extended west for a journey of twenty days. . . . My brother came back with this party, all of them with gold which they had collected in the four hours they had spent there.*

Because of its richness, Columbus decided to found a colony at the mouth of the river, which he named Santa Maria de Belén. By March, log cabins had been built, and eighty men had been selected to stay behind. By now, Columbus had given up on finding his way through to the other ocean. He was very ill, and the winds and currents were difficult to navigate. He decided to return to Spain.

The local native peoples resented the Spanish settlement, and Columbus received word that the local chief, or cacique, Quibian, was planning to raid the village and burn it down. The only solution, Christopher believed, was to capture the cacique. A raiding party was sent from the village, and Quibian and many of his men, women, and children were captured. But as they were returning the captives to the ships, Quibian escaped.

Now Christopher prepared to sail. He weighed anchor and moved his ships out of the river to a point offshore, and then he sent men back to the coast in small boats to gather wood and water for the long return journey to Spain. While the men were gone, a storm blew up and threatened the moored ships. It also kept the party onshore from returning.

The day wore on. Suddenly Christopher heard shots and yelling from up the river. A little while later, bodies of his men began to float

*On the fourth voyage, Columbus tried to establish a trading post and fort near the mouth of the Belén River. He was convinced that much gold would be found inland in the land he named Veragua. The natives, fearing that a permanent settlement would mean their enslavement, attacked some of the sailors. This woodcut shows that attack in which all but one of the sailors aboard the caravel* Capitana *were killed.*

out to sea. Christopher knew that Cacique Quibian had attacked.

When the storm was over, Christopher sent a small boat ashore to see what had happened. Most of the settlers and the ships' wood-gathering party were behind the barricades built at the fort on the banks of the Belén River. Many had been killed in the attack, and many more were wounded. Everyone wanted to return to the ship and go back to Spain. On April 16, 1502, they all boarded the ships and sailed away.

But the adventure was not over. Christopher continued to sail along the coast of Central America in hopes of finding the way around this land to the next ocean. All of the ships now leaked badly, and within a few days one was abandoned to sink. The coast still ran to the southeast, and finally Columbus decided to head away from it. On May 1, he set a course back to Hispaniola.

The weather was bad, and the ships were taking on more water. Pumps had to be worked day and night to keep the ships afloat. Christopher realized that he could not make it to Hispaniola, so he headed for Jamaica, barely making it to harbor on June 23. Now they were stranded. It was not likely that anyone would be coming to Jamaica.

Two men were selected to try to sail on to Hispaniola. The crew took two native canoes and lashed them together, gave them sails, and made other changes for the trip across the open sea. Columbus gave the men letters to the king and queen and others. They left Jamaica late in July. We will never know what adventures at sea these two men had, but they made it to Hispaniola.

Back on Jamaica, the rest of the sailors tried to live aboard the two ships, which were now low in the water. They were crowded, tired, angry, sick, and the food they got from the native people was not to their liking. Columbus had a hard time maintaining discipline.

On January 2, many of the sailors mutinied. They had decided to kill Columbus and take the two ships back out to sea. They were talked out of that, but they left the ships anyway and went to shore in search of canoes. They tried to sail away in canoes stolen from the natives, but the currents were too strong. Then they roamed the island, stealing food and generally causing problems.

Before long, the local people refused to supply any more food or water to Columbus and his survivors. But Columbus knew that, according to his almanac, an eclipse of the moon would occur in three days. He told the natives that he would pray to his God to hide the moon if they did not supply him and his men with food and water.

The villagers, of course, did not believe that this would happen, but Columbus convinced them to gather on the beach on the expected night to see for themselves. As the eclipse began to occur, and as the moon got darker and darker, the natives panicked and promised they

*At the end of the fourth voyage, Columbus and his men were marooned on the island of Jamaica. They could go no further because their ships were eaten through by "ship's worms." After several weeks, some of the men rebelled and tried to take over the island and thus force the natives to feed them. A battle between those loyal to Columbus and those who had rebelled took place. This woodcut depicts that battle.*

would do anything the admiral wanted if he would stop the moon from disappearing. Columbus then prayed to God to stop the eclipse, and, as you might well imagine, the moon slowly began to reappear as the eclipse ended. From that moment on, Columbus and his men had no problems obtaining supplies.

About the end of March, a small ship finally arrived from Hispaniola to let Columbus know that help would arrive soon. The ship was too small to take the stranded sailors back, but at least they knew that they would be rescued. Finally, on June 28, a caravel arrived to take Christopher and his men off Jamaica and back to Hispaniola. They had been marooned for more than a year. After a brief rest at Santo Domingo, Christopher, his son Ferdinand, and others who wished to return to Spain left on September 12. They got back to Sanlúcar de Barromeda near Cadiz, on November 7, 1504.

It was a sad return this time. No notice was made of the fourth voyage. Christopher was ill and would only live for another year and a half. On November 26, 1504, not quite three weeks after his return, his old friend and main supporter, Queen Isabella, died. This was a severe blow to Columbus. Queen Isabella had understood him; she had believed in his enterprise. Because of his illness, Christopher could not even attend her funeral. With Queen Isabella dead, King Ferdinand began to question what rights, privileges, and titles Christopher should hold, and what ones could be passed on to his family when he died.

In May, Christopher felt better, and he left immediately for the royal court. King Ferdinand received him and listened to his petition to settle the question on his privileges and titles. King Ferdinand offered to trade Christopher's title as governor and viceroy, for example, for extensive lands in the province of Castile. Christopher rejected the offer.

Since they could not agree on these matters, the admiral and the king agreed to have a third party, the archbishop of Seville, act as arbitrator and offer a solution that both could accept. The archbishop concluded that Columbus's privileges must be decided by skilled lawyers, and as for the question of his governorship over the lands he had discovered, the archbishop concluded that this was solely the king's decision. Christopher also asked the king to finance a fifth voyage. This the king refused to do.

## The Sons of Christopher Columbus

Both Diego and Ferdinand, the sons of Christopher, were taken to the royal court shortly after the second voyage. They were chosen to be pages to the young heir to the throne, Prince Juan. Prince Juan was younger than both the Columbus sons, but closer to the age of Ferdinand, who was about six years old. Diego would have been twelve or thirteen years old at this time. As pages, Columbus's sons were sort of a combination of playmates and royal servants to the young prince. When young Prince Juan died in 1498, Diego and Ferdinand were made pages to Queen Isabella herself. Being chosen as a page was a very important and prestigious position in the fifteenth century. A page lived at court, was under the direction of the royal family, was supported by the king and queen, and was trained in government operations. Most important, as a member of the court, a page got to know the king and queen on a personal level, a great help in establishing a career later.

When he became too old to be a page, Diego was made a soldier in the queen's bodyguard. When Queen Isabella died, he was appointed to the bodyguard of King Ferdinand. When his father Christopher died, Diego inherited all of his titles and privileges. He and the king got along very well. In 1509, Diego was made governor of the islands discovered by his father and moved with his wife to Santo Domingo. It was while he was governor that many of the beautiful buildings in historic Santo Domingo were constructed, including the Columbus Palace, which stands today as a museum.

Ferdinand left the queen's service when he was twenty-one and sailed with his father on the fourth voyage. After his father's death, Ferdinand lived in Seville, Spain, and began to collect one of the largest private libraries in Europe. He traveled to many countries, searching for rare books, and by the time he died, he had about fifteen thousand of them. Much of his time, however, he spent writing a biography of his father, one of our main sources of information about Christopher Columbus. Ferdinand never married.

Christopher followed the court as it moved from city to city even though he was now very weak from his illnesses. As he lay in his sickbed, he was visited once by his old friend and fellow explorer Amerigo Vespucci, after whom the newly discovered lands would be named because Vespucci clearly recognized them as new continents instead of a part of Asia. The German geographer Martin Waldseemüller published a new world map in 1507 and labeled the new lands as America.

One of Columbus's last letters is addressed to King Ferdinand as an appeal for his privileges and titles. He tells the king that as soon as he is well, he will again "offer you the use of my experience and

## Where Are the Bones of Columbus?

There is a great deal of confusion about where Columbus is buried today. When he died in 1506, he was buried at the Franciscan convent in Valladolid, Spain. His son Diego, however, transferred the body to the Carthusian monastery of Santa Maria de las Cuevas outside Seville in 1509. In 1541, the body was again moved, this time to the new cathedral built at Santo Domingo in Hispaniola. Two hundred fifty-four years later (1795), confusion about the true resting place of his body begins. In that year, Spain lost Hispaniola to France, and the remains of Columbus were shipped from the cathedral in Santo Domingo to Havana, Cuba. The confusion was caused by the fact that over two hundred different bodies were excavated from the cathedral in Santo Domingo, so a mistake could have been made. The bones sent to Havana may or may not have been those of Christopher Columbus. In 1877, almost a hundred years later, when the cathedral at Santo Domingo underwent extensive renovation, a small coffin was discovered with an inscription that read in part, "In here are the remains of Don Cristobal Colon, the Discoverer." An argument has raged ever since as to which are the true bones of Columbus. In 1898, the bones at Havana, Cuba, were sent to Spain, and today those remains are kept in a huge monument inside the cathedral in Seville. The bones discovered in 1877 are still in Santo Domingo where they too are contained inside a huge monument in that city's cathedral. So which are his bones? No one knows for sure.

knowledge as a sailor . . . [and] I will still be able to serve you in such a manner as no man has yet seen."

But it was not to be. On May 19, it was obvious that Christopher Columbus was going to die. He signed his will on that day, making his son Diego his sole heir. On May 20, 1506, his health took a rapid turn for the worse, and a priest was called to administer Last Rites to him. After receiving the Sacrament, he is said to have muttered these words: "Father, into thy hands I commend my spirit," and he died. His remains were buried (only temporarily) in the Franciscan monastery at Valladolid.

The conquest of the Ocean Sea and the discovery of a whole new

*Left: The monument holding Columbus's remains in Seville.*
*Right: The monument holding Columbus's remains in Santo Domingo.*

hemisphere were the results of the dream of Christopher Columbus. Others had touched the New World shores—the Irish, the Bristol sailors, the Vikings, maybe Asians and Africans, and maybe even very ancient sailors from barely remembered civilizations. But none of these encounters resulted in sustained contact, nor did they capitalize on their feats. The discoveries of Christopher Columbus led to colonization and commercial exchange. They led to further exploration and discovery. They led to new nations in North and South America and changed the political geography of the world.

The son of a Genoese cloth merchant followed his dream. Just as men today have dreamed of going to the moon, and have done so, and just as we continue to dream of visiting a million places in outer space, so Christopher dreamed of crossing the space of the Ocean Sea. The Ocean Sea was even more of an unknown in Columbus's day than the space of our Solar System is to us today.

We have the advantage of sophisticated technology—advanced telescopes, computers, new scientific theories, and proven scientific laws. Christopher had none of these things. He knew the vast space of the ocean was there. He read the theories of ancient and contemporary scientists about it. He made what observations he could of wind patterns, current patterns, and the like, but he had little technology.

The new ships, the caravels, were designed for ocean sailing, and sailors had had some experience in sailing the eastern edge of the Ocean Sea, but no one knew for sure if a person could cross the great barrier of water. In fact, the few who tried before Columbus in the fifteenth century never returned.

Christopher's feat was one of courage, scientific advancement, and an ability to make others see the potential of his discovery. The greatness of Columbus is not that he made the trip to the Americas; rather, it is that he showed others how to do it. The so-called Sea of Darkness, as the Ocean Sea was called, was no longer dark. Columbus lit the way in such a manner that others could sail the route immediately. This lighting of the way changed the course of world history.

# Chronology of Key Events

| | |
|---|---|
| 1451 | Christopher Columbus is born in Genoa, Italy, to Domenico Colombo and his wife Susanna Fontanarossa. |
| 1470–73 | Christopher voyages to Tunisian waters in service of René of Anjou. |
| 1475–76 | Christopher voyages to the island of Chios. |
| 1476 (August 13) | The *Bechalla* is sunk during battle off the coast of Portugal. Christopher goes to Lisbon after swimming to shore. |
| 1476–77 | During winter and spring, Christopher voyages to England and on to Iceland. |
| 1479 (fall) | Christopher marries Doña Felipa Moniz de Perestrello, daughter of the first governor of Porto Santo. |
| 1480–82 | Christopher and Felipa live in the Madeira Islands. Diego is born. Christopher makes many trading voyages in the near Ocean Sea to the Canaries, the Azores, and the Madeira Islands. |
| 1482–83 | Christopher travels to Africa. |

| | |
|---|---|
| 1483–84 | Felipa dies. Columbus moves back to Portugal. Christopher proposes his plan to cross the Ocean Sea to King John. |
| 1485 | Christopher and Diego move to Spain. |
| 1485–92 | Christopher lives in Spain and follows the royal court. The final battles against the Moors are fought. |
| 1488 | Ferdinand is born to Christopher and Beatriz Enríquez de Harana. |
| 1492 *(April 17)* | King Ferdinand and Queen Isabella approve Christopher's Enterprise of the Indies. |
| 1492 *(August 3)* | Columbus sails from Palos de la Frontera for Asia. Instead he found the New World. |
| 1492 *(August 8)* | Columbus arrives at Grand Canary Island for ship repairs. |
| 1492 *(September 24)* | The crew of the *Santa Maria* threatens to throw Christopher into the sea because they are afraid, tired, and wish to return to Spain. |
| 1492 *(October 12)* | After 36 days at sea, land is finally sighted at 2:00 A.M. That morning, Christopher sets foot on Guanahani, which he names San Salvador. |
| 1492 *(December 25)* | The *Santa Maria* is shipwrecked. Construction of La Navidad from the wood of the *Santa Maria* is begun. |
| 1493 *(March 15)* | Christopher and the *Niña* return to Palos de la Frontera. Captain Martín Pinzón and the *Pinta* return later the same day. |
| 1493 *(September 25)* | Christopher leaves on the second voyage to the New World from Cadiz, Spain. |
| 1494 *(January)* | Colony of La Isabela is founded. |
| 1496 *(June 11)* | Christopher returns to Cadiz, Spain, from second voyage. |
| 1498 *(May 30)* | Christopher begins the third voyage, leaving from Sanlúcar de Barrameda, Spain. |

| | |
|---|---|
| 1498<br>*(August 1)* | Trinidad and South America are found by Columbus. |
| 1500<br>*(August 23)* | Christopher is arrested by Bobadilla. |
| 1500<br>*(late October)* | Christopher returns from third voyage in chains to Cadiz, Spain. |
| 1502<br>*(May 11)* | Christopher begins his fourth and final voyage to the New World sailing from Cadiz, Spain. |
| 1502<br>*(July 30)* | Christopher arrives off the coast of Central America, modern-day country of Honduras. He proceeds to sail up and down the coast. |
| 1503<br>*(June 24)* | Christopher is marooned on Jamaica for a little over a year until June 29, 1504. |
| 1504<br>*(November 7)* | Christopher returns to Sanlúcar de Barrameda, Spain, a very sick man. |
| 1506<br>*(May 20)* | Christopher Columbus dies at Valladolid, Spain. |

# Glossary

ADMIRAL OF THE OCEAN SEA: the title given by the king and queen to Christopher Columbus upon his completion of crossing the Ocean Sea. The title made him one of the highest maritime officials in Spain and a full member of the Admiralty, a council that settled maritime disputes.

ANTIPODES: the name for creatures who lived on the opposite side of the world. "Pod" means feet and "anti" means against. Thus people on the other side of the world stand foot to foot to you.

ARAWAKS: the native peoples of the Caribbean Sea, whom Columbus encountered, who belonged to the Arawak language group. Their ancestors had migrated from northern South America over the centuries to most of the islands in that sea.

CACIQUE: the leader, or chief, of a Taino native village.

CAPTAIN GENERAL: Columbus's title on the first voyage before he became Admiral of the Ocean Sea. A Captain General was in charge of an entire fleet of ships rather than just one ship.

CARAVELS: small, fast sailing ships developed by the Portuguese. Their primary purpose was exploration, rather than the carrying of cargo. They were used to sail down the coast of Africa and out into the Ocean Sea.

CARIBBEAN SEA: the body of water off the coasts of southern North America, eastern Central America, and northern South America. It is divided from the Atlantic Ocean by the long archipelago (group of many islands) of the Greater and Lesser Antilles (the West Indies).

CARIBES: a subgroup of the Arawak language family who inhabited some of the Caribbean islands. The word "Caribbean" is derived from their name. The Caribes were noted for their cannibalism.

CIPANGU: the medieval name for the modern-day island of Japan off the coast of Asia. The goal of Columbus's first voyage was to sail west from the Canary Islands off the coast of Europe to Cipangu off the coast of Asia.

CORSAIRS: the pirates and/or their ships operating off the coast of north Africa. Corsairs made raids on cargo ships and occasionally upon the smaller islands and communities in the Mediterranean Sea.

GARDEN OF EDEN: the location/home of Adam and Eve. Most Christians in the fifteenth century believed that the garden still existed somewhere on the fringe of Asia. Columbus believed that he was close to the Garden of Eden on his third voyage. He said it would be inland from the Orinoco River in South America.

GREAT KHAN OF CHINA: Europeans began to hear stories of the wealth of Asia after the thirteenth century as more and more travelers went there and returned. Because of these travelers' tales, they believed that all of China (or Cathay as they called it) was ruled by a wealthy and powerful leader called the "Great Khan."

GUANAHANI: the native's name for the island where Columbus first landed in the New World. He called it San Salvador. The location of this island is disputed, but it is certain to be one of the islands in the Bahamas chain.

HISPANIOLA: the second largest island in the Greater Antilles just east of Cuba. Today it is divided into the countries of Dominican Republic and Haiti. It was Columbus's favorite island. It was also the place where he established the first Spanish colonies in the New World.

IMAGO MUNDI: Latin for the "image of the world." *Imago mundi* was the title of a book written by the famous Cardinal Pierre d'Ailly in the mid-fifteenth century. That book was Columbus's main source of information about the cosmology and geography of the world. D'Ailly had collected and recorded information about the earth and its environment in the *Imago mundi*. We know that Columbus read the *Imago mundi* very carefully because he made 898 marginal notations in the book.

ISLAMIC EMPIRE: the large empire of the Ottoman Turks with its capital in Constantinople (now Istanbul). The Turks held the Christian Holy Lands in the Near East and restricted Christian travel to those religious sites. They also limited trade between Europe and the Far East.

ISLE OF TILE: the name, in ancient times and in the Middle Ages, of Iceland.

LA RÁBIDA: the Franciscan monastery near Palos de la Frontera where Columbus stayed from time to time. Young Diego went there to school for a while. La Rábida was noted as both a center for missionary activity and as a center for science.

LINES OF DEMARCATION: invisible lines drawn north to south across a map of the Ocean Sea by Pope Alexander VI dividing that ocean space and all its islands and mainlands between Spain and Portugal. Because of this international agreement of lines, Portugal could only lay claim to the hump of South America, which became Brazil. Spain, on the other hand, got everything west of the line, including most of the New World.

NEWFOUNDLAND BANKS: an undersea elevation rising from the continental shelf off the coast of Canada in North America. (A "bank" in this sense is where the land under the ocean rises toward the surface.) It is one of the best fishing spots in the world.

NEW WORLD: the name Europeans gave to the western hemisphere. To them it was a whole "new world" which no one in Europe had mapped or knew existed until Columbus sailed there in 1492.

NORTH STAR: the star which was used to find the direction "north." It is in the northern sky (constellation Ursa Major), and can be found easily by following a line of sight from the lip of the Big Dipper to the first star encountered beyond the lip.

OCEAN SEA: the fifteenth-century name of what we now call the Atlantic Ocean. Before Columbus, many believed that there was only one huge land mass on the earth which was totally surrounded by an Ocean Sea.

PARIA: Ancient geographers thought that there had to be a fourth continent to balance the earth. They knew of three, Europe, Africa and Asia. Paria was the name they had given to this imagined fourth continent on the earth which should be in the southern hemisphere. When Columbus discovered South America, he named it Paria.

PILLARS OF HERCULES: prominent rock formations on each side of the Straits of Gibraltar that connect the Mediterranean Sea to the Atlantic Ocean.

QUINSAY: the fifteenth-century name of the modern city of Hangchow inside Hangchow Bay just south of Shanghai. This city was called the "City of Heaven" by Marco Polo, who described its fabulous wealth. To Europeans of the fifteenth century, Quisay was the symbol of all the wealth to be found in Asia.

STERNCASTLE: the high deck at the rear of a ship (the stern), which was enclosed by a defense wall (castle).

TAINO: the major subgroup of the Arawak language family of natives encountered by Columbus. They inhabited Cuba, Hispaniola, Jamaica, and the Bahamas. The Tainos were distinctive to Columbus because they had flat foreheads. This was due to their tradition of pressing a baby's head between two boards which artificially flattened the skull. Everyone of this cultural group was eventually killed from disease or massacred by the Spanish.

VIKINGS: medieval raiders and settlers from Scandinavia who sailed far out into the Ocean Sea in the eleventh century to establish colonies on Iceland and Greenland. Eventually, they landed on the coast of what today is Canada. Their efforts were not widely known in Europe. Since their colonies did not prosper in North America, the effort was long forgotten by the time Columbus sailed in 1492.

VINELAND: the area discovered by the Vikings on the North American coast of what today is Newfoundland. At least one Viking colony was established there, and maybe others. The Vikings came to Vineland primarily to cut lumber to take back to Greenland, since Greenland had no trees that could be used for construction.

# For Further Information

Columbus, Christopher. *The Log of Christopher Columbus.* Translated by Robert Fuson. Camden, Maine: International Marine Publishing Company, 1987. The translation used throughout this book.

Fernández-Armesto, Felipe. *Before Columbus: Exploration and Colonization from the Mediterranean to the Atlantic, 1229–1492.* Philadelphia: University of Pennsylvania Press, 1987. Particularly good on how men imagined the Ocean Sea and the expansion of Europeans into the near ocean islands before Columbus.

———. *Columbus and the Conquest of the Impossible.* London: Weidenfeld and Nicolson, 1974. An especially good biography from "The Great Explorers" series.

Hartinez-Hildalgo, Jose. *Columbus's Ships.* Barre, Massachusetts: Barre Publishers, 1966. Should be read along with the introductory material in Morison below.

*The Life of the Admiral Christopher Columbus by his son Ferdinand.* Translated by Benjamin Keen. New Brunswick, New Jersey: Rutgers University Press, 1950. The best translation of Ferdinand Colón's biography of his father.

Milanich, Jerald, and Susan Milbrath. *First Encounters: Spanish Explorations in the Caribbean and the United States, 1492–1570.* Gainesville: University of Florida Presses, 1989. An excellent collection of essays bringing together historical and archaeological research in the Caribbean.

Morison, Samuel. *Admiral of the Ocean Sea.* 2 volumes. Boston: Little, Brown and Company, 1942. Still the classic study of Christopher Columbus, written from the point of view of a scholar and sailor. Morison was an admiral in the U.S. Navy and a professor of history at Harvard University.

Weatherford, Jack. *Indian Givers: How the Indians of the Americas Transformed the World.* New York: Crown, 1988. Explores the contributions of the native peoples of the western hemisphere to the world.

# Index